"Those dealing with infertility ride an emotional roller coaster — seemingly alone. *Moments for Couples Who Long for Children* climbs in beside, rides along, and smoothes out many of the dips and turns of this difficult journey. Author Ginger Garrett is surprisingly frank and does not sugarcoat the topic with promises that dismiss the pain of those who long for children. Instead, these devotions come alongside and enter into the pain of those struggling with infertility. Each devotion is short enough to read in just minutes, yet rich with valuable support and guidance."

— CARRIE CARTER, M.D., author of *Thrive! A Woman's Guide to a Healthy Lifestyle* and *Mom's Health Matters*

"With humility and humor Ginger taps the rollercoaster emotions of infertility as only one who has been there can. She then balances the 'feelings' with the truth, wisdom, and promises of God's Word. I wholeheartedly recommend Ginger's devotional to anyone grieving to have a child while grasping to hold God's hand."

—TERRY WILLITS, founder, SenseSational Homes, Inc.

"Ms. Garrett has written a wonderful book to help couples struggling with infertility. The book does not try to explain the 'details' of infertility, but instead gives them spiritual 'moments' to draw strength and peace from. I highly recommend it."
— ANDREW A. TOLEDO, M.D., senior partner,
Reproductive Biology Associates; assistant clinical professor,
Department of Gynecology and Obstetrics,
Emory University, Atlanta, Georgia

"*Moments for Couples Who Long for Children* provides gentle, compassionate encouragement for couples struggling along the path of infertility, which the author accurately likens to a roller coaster and a military-forced march. As a spiritual friend, these devotional readings will give insight from scriptural examples, along with solid theological applications that will draw couples closer together and nearer to God. I suggest that couples read and savor this book together and find genuine comfort for their souls."
— WILLIAM R. CUTRER, M.D.,
Gheens professor of Christian ministry,
The Southern Baptist Theological Seminary;
author, *The Infertility Companion* (Zondervan, December 2003)

New Life Live! Meditations

MOMENTS FOR

COUPLES WHO

LONG *for*

CHILDREN

GINGER GARRETT

*introduction by* STEPHEN ARTERBURN

NAVPRESS®

BRINGING TRUTH TO LIFE

*God's Peace to you —* (handwritten)

*Ginger Garrett* (handwritten signature)

NAVPRESS
P.O. BOX 35001,
COLORADO SPRINGS, CO 80935

The Navigators is an international Christian organization. Our mission is to reach, disciple, and equip people to
know Christ and to make Him known through successive generations. We envision multitudes of diverse people
in the United States and every other nation who have a passionate love for Christ, live a lifestyle of sharing
Christ's love, and multiply spiritual laborers among those without Christ.

NavPress is the publishing ministry of The Navigators. NavPress publications help believers learn biblical truth
and apply what they learn to their lives and ministries. Our mission is to stimulate spiritual formation among
our readers.

Published in association with the literary agency of Alive Communications, Inc., 7680 Goddard Street, Suite
200, Colorado Springs, CO 80920.
ISBN 1-57683-472-7

Cover design by David Carlson Design
Cover illustration: Boden/Ledingham Masterfile
Creative Team: Dan Rich, Steve Halliday, Debby Weaver, Darla Hightower, Glynese Northam

Some of the anecdotal illustrations in this book are true to life and are included with the permission of the per-
sons involved. All other illustrations are composites of real situations, and any resemblance to people living or
dead is coincidental.

Garrett, Ginger, 1968-
  Moments for couples who long for children / Ginger Garrett.
    p. cm. -- (New life live devotional series)
  ISBN 1-57683-472-7
  1. Infertility--Religious aspects--Christianity. 2. Consolation. I.
Title. II. Series.
  RC889.G35 2003
  362.1´96692--dc21

                        2003010685

Printed in Canada

1 2 3 4 5 6 7 8 9 10 / 07 06 05 04 03

FOR A FREE CATALOG OF
NAVPRESS BOOKS & BIBLE STUDIES,
CALL 1-800-366-7788 (USA)
OR 1-416-499-4615 (CANADA)

*For Sherrill, and for everyone who waits for a child.*
*You are all in my heart, and my prayers.*

# Contents

# ACKNOWLEDGMENTS

I am a blessed woman. I have a husband who believed in the vision for this book and encourages me to live outside my comfort zone, every day. For better, for worse, and for every moment in between, I love you.

And I have parents, family, and friends who have made even the most unbearable moments tolerable. I'll always remember my thirtieth birthday with you all. I had just learned I was finally pregnant—and miscarrying. You all gathered on that icy, dark evening and lit my home with love. Phone calls from my family tied up our line, and we all raised our glasses (of cider!) and toasted one of the few certainties I had: that my life was blessed because I was loved by God and by each of you as well.

# INTRODUCTION

I love children. My heart leaps at the thought of a young baby in my arms or a small child playing at the beach, experiencing the wonder of God's world. The laughter of a child is my music. It has always been that way for me and when I left college I left with a degree in Elementary Education. I just wanted to be with great kids and have the opportunity to make them greater. My time teaching fifth graders was some of the most enriching and fulfilling of my life.

When I married Sandy I looked forward to us having children. I could not wait to be a father. But I had to wait because shortly after we were married we discovered that we were an infertile couple. We tried all of the "fertility rights" of the medical profession and every one of them failed. A new month would come full of hope and promise until the irrefutable evidence would surface that once again we were not going to have a baby. There was no need to linger as we walked by another baby store full of furniture and equipment we did not need. The pain was deep and the despair engulfed me, the man whom I thought was born to be a dad. My wife did not share much of her feelings with me, but I know how horribly empty she must have felt in the sisterhood of infertility. It showed in every interaction she had with me and with others.

I must assume that if you are reading this introduction you are one of us who has longed for children and for some time been denied. I hope you know that you are not alone and that others suffer and struggle as you. If you are like me, you are amazed at how insensitive the world can be to our longing for a child. Shallow comments and superficial remarks that only made the pain worse was what I got from most people. I did not want to hear anyone's explanation of why this was happening or what God was trying to do in me through this. I just wanted a baby and every day without a child was an incomplete day. And on Father's Day I was anywhere but in church where others were celebrating what I longed for.

If your journey is anything like mine, I believe these devotionals are going to be a comfort to you and enrich your spirit. There are no sermons in these pages, just some deep thoughts and keen insights from Ginger Garrett who has been where you are. There is wisdom here for you directly from God's Word without a hint of condemnation, because in Christ there is none. There is also a sense of hope that comes from these moments with God that Ginger has directed. This hope can be your anchor to a life where you start to enjoy children in a new way. It is the hope of healing so that you can take pleasure in God's children even if they do not carry your genes.

I do not know your future, but I know God has one for you that is rich in his love and blessings. He may bless you with an adopted child as he did me. Madeline is such a joy to me that if conceiving a child would have meant not being her dad, I would not have wanted to conceive. You may not adopt and your blessing from God may come in some other way and that way may never include the words Daddy or Mommy. If that is God's path, I hope that you will walk it in strength and understanding and that these devotionals will help you grow in God's grace along your way.

With deep love and compassion for you,
*Stephen Arterburn*
FOUNDER, NEW LIFE MINISTRIES

# FEAR OF THE FUTURE

*The LORD himself goes before you and will be with you;*
*he will never leave you nor forsake you.*
*Do not be afraid; do not be discouraged.*

DEUTERONOMY 31:8

After we had been married for a bit, my husband and I decided to start our family. We bought a house and chose the room that would one day become the nursery. One morning, while alone in the house, I knelt to say a prayer of dedication in this room. We had felt so giddy with our plans and purchases that I felt we had almost left God out of the process. So there I knelt, saying a quick prayer of thanksgiving for the child that was sure to come, and asking God to bless my timeline.

God spoke to me very clearly and quite suddenly. I didn't hear an audible voice or see God in the room, but His words spoke unmistakably in my heart. "This is out of your control," they seemed to say.

The message both shocked and puzzled me. I had expected to be blessed, to have my plan stamped and approved — and God was telling me it was out of my control? I not only didn't understand the message, I didn't like it. But He revealed nothing more to me, and so my husband and I continued on our plan to start a family.

When we conceived just three months later, we felt overjoyed. Our lives seemed to be unfolding according to plan, and we had no fear of the future. *If this is out of my control,* I thought, *it sure is turning out according to my plan!* In my quiet time during the mornings, when I read my Bible and prayed, I felt repeatedly drawn to Deuteronomy 31:8. Yet this puzzled me — why should it have special meaning for me? After all, with my life unfolding so perfectly, what did I have to fear? And why would I be discouraged? I was getting everything I wanted, when I wanted it.

Days later I suffered a head-on car accident that totaled my car. As the ultrasound technician passed the sonogram wand over my belly, her face revealed the terrible truth. The baby was gone. At that moment I was initiated into a sorority I never wanted to join: the group of women who have lost children before their time. The weeks that followed brought more shocks — my body refused to heal after the loss and doctors discovered a birth defect in my reproductive system that meant I might never have another chance to conceive.

I clung to the verse from Deuteronomy. What a comfort that Jesus had known my future before I did and that He always stayed ahead of me, laying a foundation of comfort and encouragement. Yet at the same time He remained with me, holding my hand. One day I had been an expectant mother; the next, I became a barren woman. Jesus knew and had been preparing me to face the trial.

The same is true for you. There is no situation in your future that Jesus has not already seen. Even now He is preparing blessings of peace and comfort for each hour of trial you will face.

———————

*Lord, having a child is out of our control, yet You ask us to not be afraid nor discouraged — and this is so hard! We don't know what the future holds and we feel so helpless over the events yet to unfold. You've seen our future and You tell us we don't need to feel fear or discouragement. Please help make that a reality for us today! Give us confidence and encouragement.*

# A SISTERHOOD OF INFERTILITY

*Therefore, since we are surrounded by such a great cloud of witnesses,*
*let us throw off everything that hinders and the sin that so easily entangles,*
*and let us run with perseverance the race marked out for us.*

HEBREWS 12:1

How many women in the Bible struggled with infertility?

- The mother of Samson, whose son performed amazing feats of strength and courage.
- Elizabeth, mother of John the Baptist, a prophet who prepared the people for Christ's arrival.
- Sarah, mother of Isaac, from whom the nation of Israel sprang.
- Rebekah, mother of Jacob and Esau.
- Hannah, mother of the godly prophet, Samuel.
- Rachel, mother of Joseph, who would save a nation from famine.

Each of these women, though barren for many years, changed history forever by waiting for God's answer. The Bible spotlights many stories of mothers who had no hope of conception — until God intervened. Although the Lord never reveals why they had to wait, it always amazes me to read about the child for whom they were waiting.

In the lives of these women, infertility amounted to an invitation for God to act. God used these women to accomplish great things. In fact, conception despite long infertility held such importance in God's eyes that He often sent an angel to make the birth announcement. A surprising number of the Bible's angelic proclamations announce the end of a woman's infertility and reveal a pending miracle in God's plan.

These women endured the agony of waiting and the heartache of feeling the dream of children slip through their fingers. Hannah grieved with such force that a priest who saw her praying mistakenly thought her drunk! Ultimately, God answered each of their prayers as a unique part of His plan for their lives and for the world.

God is not blind to barrenness. The Bible repeatedly proves that not only is He aware, but He is actively bringing about His plan for our lives — even when we lose all hope. When you feel the despair or hopelessness of fighting a battle that seems to have no end in sight, picture yourself surrounded by this "great cloud of witnesses." Picture them cheering you on as you handle your infertility with hope, faith, and love.

---

*Thank you, Lord, that You surround us with stories of hope and faithful perseverance. Help me take comfort in knowing that You honored these women as they waited for Your answer. It gives me such hope to know that You chose barren women to give birth to such important people in Your plan!*

# AN IDENTITY TO KEEP

*Whoever finds his life will lose it,*
*and whoever loses his life for my sake will find it.*

MATTHEW 10:39

I never thought of my identity as wrapped up in my ability to conceive a child — until the doctors told me I couldn't get pregnant. I remember going home that day and staring at my reflection in the mirror. In one afternoon the plans for the next half of my life derailed.

I stared at my image, at a loss for who I was to become and how I was going to fill my years. *What now,* I wondered, *and more importantly, who will I become? If I won't become a mother, who will I be?*

I tried to pray, but received no answers from heaven. My mind began to wander, and I tried to answer the questions myself.

First, I flirted with the idea of plastic surgery, a total overhaul. If my body wouldn't function right, it might as well look good. But as I began tallying all the procedures necessary to bring me even close to perfection, my inspiration quickly faded. Too much work to be done, and not enough money! Besides, the battle against infertility had sapped me of so much emotional energy that I wasn't sure I could even muster up the excitement to say goodbye to my thighs. More importantly, though, I had just gone through five months of diagnostic surgeries and procedures, and I didn't feel eager to spend any more time in a doctor's office.

Then I thought about quitting my career. I could devote myself to my garden, my animals, and volunteer work — but the idea of living alone all day in a house with an empty nursery seemed too depressing.

And so ideas from the mundane to the wildly irresponsible came and went throughout that afternoon and the following months. And still no clear answer came to my identity crisis. God didn't grant me a bold new vision of who I was to become. I could only allow time to pass and wait for God to reveal the next chapter in my story.

Romans 12:1 tells us to offer our bodies as sacrifices to God. The text lists no exclusions or limitations for this sacrifice, based on what our bodies can or cannot do. God asks each of us to present our bodies as an offering to Him. I wanted my body to perform so that I could fulfill my identity in becoming a mother. God wanted me to entrust my body, with all its flawed physical processes and weaknesses, to Him.

In addition, Matthew 10:39 instructs me to lose my life, or my idea of my life, for His sake. In return, God promised to reveal to me a true, unshakable identity.

God promises you, too, that if you will lay your body and your agenda at His feet as a daily, living sacrifice, He will make you vibrantly alive. And then your identity will be as certain, secure, and startlingly beautiful as you can imagine.

---

*Lord, it's easy to grasp intellectually that we are more than our bodies; but when our bodies fail us, it profoundly affects us. It seems as if our bodies can dictate who we become. We want to trust in You, and yet we can't help but let our minds wander into the future and wonder who we will be. Help us to remember to present our bodies as sacrifices to You; we are not responsible for what they can or cannot do. Our only role is to lay them at Your feet and wait for You to give us new meaning.*

# OF DOGS AND PIGS

*Do not give dogs what is sacred; do not throw your pearls to pigs.*
*If you do, they may trample them under their feet,*
*and then turn and tear you to pieces.*

MATTHEW 7:6

Infertility draws upon all of your resources — especially discretion. Some people you can trust with the intimate details of your life; some you cannot. God wants to protect you, so He encourages you to carefully observe the behavior of friends before you trust them with your most private thoughts.

The Bible frankly refers to certain untrustworthy people as dogs, and others as pigs. There is a clear difference, I believe, between the two groups. That difference lies in their intention to hurt or help us when they break our confidence.

As a dog lover, I understand that while dogs are generally well-intentioned, they also are inherently unable to handle certain precious possessions. In this sense, a "dog" might be a well-meaning friend who cannot keep a secret. This can include even Christian friends who might share your private struggles in the guise of asking others to pray.

Pigs, on the other hand, act maliciously. Pigs befriend and

listen to you, but at the right time, they turn and rip you to pieces. Do you know anyone who loves to lash out at others behind their backs and reveal their secrets? That person has a distinctive spiritual smell about them, unpleasantly reminiscent of the pigsty.

God will ultimately deal with both groups, judging them by their intentions as well as their actions. But regardless of that judgment, He warns us that nothing good can come from sharing precious things with either pigs or dogs.

Infertility is a lonely business, and often there are no easy answers. Our good judgment can get overruled at times by our need to receive comfort and companionship. It may feel more tempting to pour out our heart to a person present and in the flesh than to an invisible God. But God wants to protect us from unnecessary heartache as we wait for a child. Therefore, He instructs us to survey the people around us and wisely choose whom to trust with personal information.

———

*Lord, it surprises us to hear You talk so frankly about people! But You're right — there are people I need to watch out for, especially when I am vulnerable and needy. Please keep my spiritual eyes open and help me to seek out and find the right people with whom I can share the intimate details of my life. Infertility can be lonely, and I may feel tempted to reveal too much simply because someone seems willing to listen. I will trust in You to deal with the pigs and dogs in my life as You see fit and in Your time. Until then, remind me when to keep my mouth shut. And please surround me with godly, trustworthy friends.*

# FORGIVING CRUEL REMARKS

*Jesus said, "Father, forgive them,*
*for they do not know what they are doing."*

LUKE 23:34

Can you name every insensitive thing said to you about infertility and conception? I can. Those careless words, rarely intended to hurt, seemed to sear themselves into my brain. A woman once suggested that I had some hidden sin in my life and that I would at last become pregnant when I confessed and repented. A different woman at my office shared horror stories of "a friend of a friend" who exhausted her marriage and bank account to become pregnant, only to wind up alone and bankrupt.

Infertile couples certainly are not alone, of course, in suffering through well-intentioned insults. One woman whose daughter had committed suicide by hanging herself received a sympathy card showing a cartoon animal dangling by its neck from a tree. The caption read, "Hang in There!" Anyone who has suffered a tragedy or life-changing illness probably can recount hurtful stories of unintentional blunders by well-meaning people.

Yet friends and loved ones rarely mean to hurt us with their words. Often at a loss about what to say — and uncomfortable with silence — they just say whatever comes to mind. Others who wound us carelessly may have no idea that we're struggling to conceive.

So how should we respond? Should we retaliate? Most of us have many ways of retaliating. Repeating the offense in the form of gossip gives us an indirect means of retaliation. Lashing out verbally or criticizing the offender provides a more straightforward approach.

As Jesus hung on a cross, crucified by those who rejected Him as Savior, He did neither. He spoke not a word of retaliation. Jesus did not attempt to justify Himself to them or even try to respond to their insults with the truth. Instead, He spoke of forgiveness. "Father," He said, "forgive them, for they do not know what they are doing." We may want to retaliate — but in fact, retaliating will only drive others away at the very time we most need their prayers and encouragement. Jesus calls us to forgive instead.

If you want to imitate Christ's example, you must forgive *even before you're asked*. Also ask God to forgive the offender. Then try to lovingly explain what words hurt and how friends and loved ones can best support you. Many people simply don't know how to respond to suffering; forgiveness frees you to guide them from hurting to helping.

Try to realize, too, that you may be guilty of the same offenses. There have been times in the past and there will surely be times in the future when you will say or do the wrong thing, despite the best of intentions. Wouldn't you want to know that your friend judged you by your good intentions instead of your hurtful blunders?

---

*Lord, even as You died on the cross for us, we said things
to intentionally hurt You and cause You pain. And yet
You forgave us, before we asked and before we cared.
Please show me how to forgive those who hurt me, too,
before they ask and before they even realize what they've
done. I trust You to teach them how to be sensitive to
those who hurt, just as You are teaching me.*

# TRUST IN THE LORD

*When I am afraid, I will trust in you. In God, whose word I praise,*
*in God I trust; I will not be afraid. What can mortal man do to me?*

PSALM 56:3-4

I laid on the cold, steel table as the machines hummed and purred, displaying an outline of my entire reproductive system on the screen just above me. Two doctors in the room surveyed the results of this test, a hysterosalpingogram. The dimmed lights matched the hushed voices. Suddenly (and loudly) one doctor exploded, "Well, *she'll* never get pregnant!"

I would like to tell you that I had a snappy comeback ready, or even a biting Bible verse, but I felt too stunned and heartsick to react. And then things got worse.

The rude doctor ran from the room, exclaiming that he needed to find another doctor — any doctor would do — who wanted to come see the incredibly deformed uterus appearing onscreen.

I plunged into a state of chaos and uncertainty. I had gone in for the test to get some answers and instead felt like I had been given a life sentence.

"No hope for you," he declared.

I can still hear that doctor's words. His years of medical school and residencies, his years of seeing patients and reading complicated tests, had given him the authority to state an informed medical opinion. Opinions, however — even the most respected ones — mean nothing if they conflict with God's purpose in your life. Doctors may offer medical opinions, but they can never foretell the future. How and when and whether you will have children is at the sole discretion of your Lord. Only God can determine your future — not a medical test, or a lab result, or even a highly renowned doctor.

So trust in the Lord, and do not be afraid.

---

*Lord, my heart yearns for a child, and sometimes I feel I am at the mercy of the doctors, not You. Please remind me today that only You hold my future. I do not know how You will overcome the obstacles in my path, or how You will strengthen me for the journey ahead, but I will put my trust in You, and You alone. Help me to seek the wisest of medical counsel and yet always remember that You are wiser still. Others may try to write the story for me, but only You script the ending.*

# NO REASON FOR SHAME

*I sought the LORD, and he answered me;*
*he delivered me from all my fears. Those who look to him are radiant;*
*their faces are never covered with shame.*

PSALM 34:4-5

Couples who have no trouble conceiving often flaunt their fertility as if it were a measure of their worth. How, then, are "the barren" not supposed to feel *un*worthy?

While I underwent fertility treatments and suffered through miscarriages, a close friend got pregnant, time after time, "without trying." She began decorating her house with statues of pregnant women. She and her husband proudly boasted about her fertility. So if they could proudly boast of their fertility, should I hide and feel ashamed of my infertility?

What about you? Do you ever feel awkward and embarrassed about your season of waiting when in the company of couples with children? Do you sometimes feel ashamed that you cannot do what seems so natural and easy for everyone else? Let me ask you a question that I had to answer many times myself: *Whose idea was this?* Did you ask for this delay, for the heartache and the frustration? Of course not! This season of waiting is part of God's plan for your life; it is not your own scheme. We do not know why God has chosen to allow some of us to wait while He allows others to conceive immediately. Children are a blessing from God, the Bible says (see Psalm 127:3-5), but they are not His *only* blessing. Nor are they necessarily a sign of His favor.

Fertility and children should never be confused with God's stamp of approval on a life. The evening news can provide plenty of examples of ungodly, undeserving men and women who nevertheless have been blessed with children.

We know that God is loving and gracious and will provide for our yearning for a child in His way and in His time. We do not need to feel ashamed of His plan for our life, even when it carries us down paths we would have chosen to avoid. There is great honor in waiting when it is God's plan for you.

---

*Lord, sometimes I feel cheated and even ashamed that I cannot do something that I think should be so natural and easy. I feel somehow that I have let my spouse down or that my body has let me down. I feel ashamed that I don't "measure up" when I am around couples with children. Please teach me to look to You and let my face radiate with Your light and peace. Remind me that this, too, is part of Your plan for my life — at least for the moment — and that You are a trustworthy God! Teach me to honor You through this season of waiting and give me courage as I surrender my life's course to You.*

# IS BIOLOGY DESTINY?

*I am the LORD, the God of all mankind. Is anything too hard for me?*

JEREMIAH 32:27

Do you feel inadequate for the tasks to which God has called you? God expects great things of us, but He rarely equips us in the ways we would choose.

Although Moses suffered from a speech impediment, God called him to be His prophet to Pharaoh. Moses had to address the most powerful ruler on earth at that time, in front of scores of government officials and dignitaries.

The apostle Paul suffered from a physical ailment that often pained him, a "thorn" which he repeatedly asked God to remove. Instead, God promised to sustain Paul with His grace and called him to a physically rigorous life. The Lord did not appear to make any concessions for Paul's infirmity.

While God did not give either man the physical traits or abilities that seemed best suited to their destinies, the Lord still expected great things from both men — and in fact had prepared great deeds for them to accomplish.

It is human nature to point to our inadequacies and let them direct us down the path of least resistance. Darwin believed biology is destiny. According to Darwin, our biology (with all its limitations) directs the course of our lives — certainly not deity. Darwin no doubt would find it hard to believe that a stuttering man like Moses could be heard plainly both in Egypt and across the ages. He would make no exception for a man like Paul, who despite pain and hunger and shipwrecks and exhaustion, could be remarkably used by God to shape the look and mission of the church.

I think of another person created by God who seemed woefully ill-equipped for his divine destiny. In 1770 a baby boy was taking shape in his mother's womb, a lad who one day would become perhaps the greatest composer of all time. God oversaw every detail of his development, gifting him with genius, passion, and a relentless drive to express the majesty of life through music. God did not, however, grant the boy the gift of permanent hearing.

We don't know if Beethoven ever wept over this refusal. We do know that at the end of his life he composed the famous piece, "Ode to Joy." A man denied his most crucial physical ability ached not with sorrow and regret, but with passion for life and joy. Beethoven reached beyond his physical limitations to compose music that would enrich concert halls and homes for hundreds of years to come. His biology did not determine his destiny after all.

Our limitations do not speak of our capabilities — they only whisper of what God can overcome.

---

*Lord, we want to be parents, and yet it seems we cannot conceive. We feel imprisoned by the bodies You have given us, and yet You have told us to "be fruitful and multiply." Please, Lord, help us to trust in Your plan, even when it seems there's been some mistake. Help us to see You triumphing over the physical limitations we face. Show us a destiny that does not depend on what our bodies can accomplish.*

# YOU'RE IN THE ARMY NOW!

*For I am the* LORD, *your God, who takes hold of your right hand*
*and says to you, Do not fear; I will help you.*

ISAIAH 41:13

New recruits to the armed services go on torturous marches, carry
heavy gear on their backs, and often walk through terrible conditions. They can't stop, get precious few rest stops, and no one asks
how they feel about the journey. Recruits who cannot complete
the march suffer shame and humiliation and often get discharged
from service.

You, too, may feel as though you've been drafted against your
will into the long march of infertility. Suddenly you're sloshing
through unpleasant conditions, heavy burdens weighing down
your shoulders.

Are you short of breath, worn out, and unsure whether to go
on? Should you give up and accept defeat? If so, you may have
reached what military recruits call The Hump, the critical junction where you choose between defeat or against-all-odds
endurance. Recruits know that although they face a great battle
of physical endurance, the battle for their minds to stay the
course is even greater.

Our testing ground is spiritual as well as mental. We can choose to sit down in despair and defeat, exclaiming that God cannot love us if He has allowed this march against our will and amid these terrible conditions. Or we can choose to give away our agenda and give up our fears — into the hands of a loving God. We can decide to trust Him for the final outcome, regardless of what that might be.

If you have reached The Hump, you are nearing the end of your own power. You cannot complete this march relying on your own ability and with your own resources. You will feel tempted to plop down, to quit trying for a child, and to give up on God entirely. You can choose to stop this relentless march. You can weep for what you do not have and what has not been done and leave behind your faith in a just and loving God. Or you can walk on, receiving your strength from the outstretched arms of an unseen but ever-faithful God. God asks that we continue this march only on the promise that He is good and that He will provide whatever we need, when we need it.

You can end this march in one of two ways. Retreat and never conquer — or abandon the weight of fears and personal agendas and resolutely walk on in faith. The choice is yours.

———

*Lord, when we grow tired and do not know if we should*
*quit or continue, please allow us rest and refreshment.*
*Encourage us and give us strength. Increase our faith so*
*that we can believe in Your overwhelming love and*

*direction more than we believe in the apparent reality of
our circumstances. Help us not to focus in anger at the
circumstances or the seeming injustice of being forced
into this march against our will. If we have to choose
between asking You for the strength to endure and questioning You about Your methods, grant us trust and
power to choose the former!*

# FEAR OF THE UNKNOWN

*The secret things belong to the LORD our God.*

DEUTERONOMY 29:29

Our suffering can increase through the agony of not knowing when it will end and why God has allowed it. We want answers to questions that God does not seem eager to explain. We struggle with the intense desire to know when we will finally have a child; we can bear any temporary delay. We imagine that if only God would tell us the day and time that our wait will end, we could relax and pace ourselves during our waiting.

But the idea that this suffering could stretch on indefinitely haunts us and makes the present much more difficult. We can stand short bursts of pain, such as in the dentist's chair or when we get a flu shot, because we know the pain will end quickly and because we feel confident the suffering will produce a greater good. We don't seem to need, or ask for, God's strength in those moments.

So long as we understand why we must suffer, we don't much search for God's presence in the pain. So long as we know the height, depth, and length of our suffering, we can rely on our own strength to bring about our desire and meet the demands of the crisis. Information becomes control.

Lack of control, however, with no sense of when the suffering will end or why God allows it, nudges us to an all-knowing, all-powerful Lord. God can best demonstrate who He is when we are paying careful attention. Perhaps this is one reason why He does not reveal to us His exact times and dates and reasons. We want Him to reveal the future — He wants to reveal His character.

---

*Lord, teach us to cling to You! Bless our waiting by revealing glimpses of Your love for us. Show us how powerful You are, above any circumstance or enemy that threatens us. As we wait for Your deliverance, help us to trust You for the exact date and time that our suffering will end. Help us to trust You with the question of "why." Grant us the courage to embrace the chaos and confusion of our suffering, knowing that You remain in control and never out of reach.*

# THE NEED FOR PATIENCE

*But those who hope in the LORD will renew their strength.*
*They will soar on wings like eagles; they will run and not grow weary,*
*they will walk and not be faint.*

ISAIAH 40:31

No couple facing infertility can make it without patience. If you already have patience, you'll need more. If you don't have patience, you'll have to develop it . . . and quickly!

Infertility brings so many frustrating delays: waiting for test results; the right time of the month; doctor's appointments; answers to prayers. Your whole being — spirit, body, and soul — can become weary from waiting, impatient for the final outcome to be revealed. Your body needs physical patience for the endless tests, procedures, and monthly cycles of trying to conceive. Your soul needs emotional patience to handle the roller coaster of hope and disappointment, daydreams, and frustrating realities. Your spirit needs supernatural patience for the endless challenges to your faith.

Daily you are asked to wade through difficult circumstances without blaming the all-powerful God who chooses to let you continue on this journey. Patience grows your faith, helping you to see that your journey is leading to something wonderful prepared for you by God Himself. Faith enables you to continue to pray when no answers come.

Isaiah 40:31 reminds us that we get fresh strength every time we put our hope in God. This is the strength that fuels our patience and grows our faith. Sometimes we get to soar above our problems. Sometimes God lets us quickly run through the difficulties. And sometimes, although we may hate it, God asks us to walk. Each step seems slow and deliberate, yet He promises to give us the endurance to complete the journey day by day.

An old proverb states, "In God's economy, nothing is wasted." The time you spend waiting today can become the critical time God uses to prepare you for the answers to your prayers. God remains constantly at work in us and around us. No matter how He moves you through your difficult today — soaring above, running through, or simply plodding along — may God grant you the patience and endurance to renew your strength as you hope in Him to answer your heartfelt prayers.

---

*Lord, we want to soar like the eagles and run without growing weary. Walking seems so frustratingly slow! We just want to cross the finish line — but You have many plans to accomplish through our gradual progress. Give us endurance! The journey can feel so long and confusing; sometimes it can be hard to see Your hand in our circumstances. Grant us the patience to continue walking, give us the strength to keep moving, and grow our faith in You with every delay as we wait for a child.*

# WHEN THE ANSWER IS NO

*The LORD binds up the bruises of his people and heals the wounds he inflicted.*

ISAIAH 30:26

You waited until the appointed day to do the pregnancy test. You bit your nails and tried to restrain the growing fantasies of how you would announce the glorious news.

. . . And then the pregnancy test came back negative.

Or perhaps after undergoing yet another procedure, hoping that *this* time things would work out, the doctor entered the room and said, "I'm sorry, but there's nothing further we can do for you."

You've trusted God with your deepest longings to have a child. You've submitted to all the tests, procedures, delays and disappointments. You've read the Bible and have gone to church. You continued to patiently ask for a child — and God answered, "No."

When I have felt the bitter sting of "No," I've lashed out at God, hurling my accusations at Him — only to be met with silence, the same creeping, awful silence that met my endless prayers for a child. My anger seemed as impotent to move God into action as were my repeated prayers.

What does God say we should do when He answers with "No"?

When heartbreak sends us reeling, does the Bible offer us any instruction?

It does — but I'll warn you, it's strange. The Bible tells us to praise Him (as illogical and infuriating as that may seem). We may not feel thankful for our situation, but we can express our thanks for what God can do through it. God has no trouble working miracles in unexpected ways and at unlikely moments.

Just as we know God exists, even when all the evidence of our lives seems to point the other way, so we know God can grant us a child even when all the evidence runs contrary to that possibility. God loves to give us incredible glimpses into His nature when the line breaks between what we want and what He has chosen to provide.

Second, the Bible instructs us to pour out our hearts to God, telling Him everything, even our shameful thoughts of discouragement and doubt. Isaiah 30:26 promises that "the LORD binds up the bruises of his people and heals the wounds he inflicted."

Finally, we are called once more to wait. God promises us that we will not mourn forever. Every grief has its season, and it will pass as surely as snow melts into spring. Of course, God may also allow us to weep for a night, a time so blackened with tears, envy, rage, and disappointment that we feel almost engulfed. But God promises that a morning of rejoicing lies ahead, a sweet dawn of unexpectedly tender mercies and blessed deliverance.

---

*Lord, when Your answer is "no," it crushes us. We often plunge into a night of bitter grief and tears. But You have more planned for us just ahead, a bright morning of rejoicing. When we see nothing to rejoice over, remind us that we have not yet reached the end of our journey, even if Your answer today is "no." You are leading us into a new place, a place we could never have imagined before we began our pursuit of parenthood. Help us to trust You, to want to be where You lead! Help us to trust You with the bitter disappointments and the lonely silences, and help us to believe You will yet give us a reason to rejoice.*

# HAPPY ENDINGS

*They will proclaim his righteousness to a people yet unborn — for he has done it.*
PSALM 22:31

When the doctors told me I would never have children, I remember praying in a dazed state of mind, my heart suddenly aware of all the suffering around me. I realized for the first time how many people hurt from infertility and how deep the pain can go. I promised God that I would gladly serve him in ministering to women who suffer from infertility. If God chose to let me remain childless, I would serve Him with all my might to minister to others who were hurting as I was.

It sounds like a spiritual decision, doesn't it? But actually it was self-serving. I felt angry — furious, in fact — that life could strip a dream away so callously. I determined to strike back. If I had to suffer, it would not be in vain. As a rebellious person by nature, I decided to somehow limit the hold infertility could have on my life.

As time went on, however, I really began to believe that God would use me to serve others and that He would also enable me to become a mother. I left wide open the possibilities of how this might occur. Although I felt that someday I would indeed have a child, I trusted God to enable me to mother in any way He saw fit — whether through adoption, caring for children in the community, or becoming involved in church ministries. Again, it sounds very spiritual — but again, I felt afraid to get my hopes up that I could get pregnant. I was "leaving it all in the Lord's hands," all right — but only because I felt too scared to trust and hope.

Praise the Lord that He doesn't wait to bless us until we're spiritually perfect! Riddled with rebellion and plagued by fear, I still prayed and waited for God to act. Psalm 22:31 became a promise for my life that I clutched to when my spirit sank into despair. I pictured myself as an old woman, telling the children around me about God's faithfulness during a time of great struggle. This verse also encouraged me because it reminded me that God already had acted. He already had answered my prayers, although I couldn't see His answer just yet. I wasn't waiting for God to make up his mind to act — I was waiting to see how His mercy would unfold.

Do you have a verse for your life to remind you of the happy ending to your story? Pick one out today and read it as often as possible. The Psalms provide a great place to look. Find a verse that reminds you how God has answered your prayers in a loving, faithful way, something that gives you reason to praise Him all your life. No matter what's in your heart — no matter how far away from God you feel — don't hesitate to approach Him and let Him sort out all the details of your life. He is faithful and has blessings in store for those who dare ask what He can do.

Lord, sometimes we feel so powerless as we wait to see how our story will turn out. The uncertainty of our situation can make us doubt Your love for us and what sort of God you must be to allow such suffering. Please guide me to a verse in the Bible that can speak to my hope in You and in Your goodness.

# PURPOSE IN LIFE

*The LORD will fulfill his purpose for me.*

PSALM 138:8

Infertility can turn your world upside down. It can derail your plans, causing you to feel helpless to get back on track. You may question your purpose in life, wondering what you are meant to do if children are not in your future (or at least not in your immediate future). Depression can overwhelm you as you scramble to adjust to this unwelcome dissolution of your plans and dreams.

God's Word promises us that, however we feel, we *do* have a heavenly purpose and God *will* fulfill it. That purpose might differ from the one you've designed for yourself, or it may be the same but with a different timeline. Because God has a purpose planned for you and for this suffering, you have no responsibility to create the purpose or bring it to pass. You are responsible only to look to God for guidance as He reveals His purpose for your life, and then act in obedience to this calling and to His Word.

Your life has purpose, and this purpose remains despite your current crisis of infertility. In fact, it may well be that this crisis forms a large part of God's purpose for you. Throughout the Bible, suffering became the catalyst for dynamic healing and spiritual growth. When we suffer, we are more likely to turn to God and willingly to follow His leading. We become much more likely to listen and obey when we believe God can grant us relief. God, in His mercy, will not allow our sorrows to be wasted. He promises that we won't suffer in vain if we turn to Him in our heartache.

The victory of Jesus on the cross means that we are not bound by apparent reality, but by Truth. What seems to be the end is only the beginning. What enemies intended to use to break our hearts becomes the very thing that brings healing and opens our mouths wide in joyful song. The piercing loneliness of infertility becomes a blessing as God reveals incredible comforts and helps us in turn to comfort others. God is shaping you for a great purpose — *His* purpose, and you can find strength for the battle today by remembering that He *will* fulfill this vision!

---

*Lord, perhaps we can't see Your clear purpose in our*
*waiting for a child, but it eases our pain to know You do*
*indeed have a plan. Help us to remember that every little*
*obstacle, every lonely week that passes and every month*
*that disappoints us is moving us toward the fulfillment of*
*Your plan, not away from it.*

# CHOOSING THE RIGHT ROUTE

*I am the LORD your God, who teaches you what is best for you,*
*who directs you in the way you should go.*

ISAIAH 48:17

When you face a crisis, people will often tell you to "surrender" and to trust the Lord. But what does this mean when the crisis is infertility? Should you avoid doctors and medical treatments and expect the Lord to heal you without outside intervention? Does it reveal a lack of faith if you use fertility drugs or medical procedures to try to become pregnant?

Nowhere in the Bible does God condemn doctors or technology. God does, however, condemn putting our faith in anyone or anything but Him. On the other hand, the Lord does not and cannot look favorably on technologies that treat with disrespect the preciousness of unborn life. Procedures that try to "create" embryos call for special attention and vigilance. If you are asking God to create a life within you, you must make sure that any medical intervention does not destroy the life you've begged for.

The root of the issue becomes this: Where is your hope? Remember, God alone can grant you children. God can bring about His plan for your life whether or not you opt for medical assistance.

Isaiah 48:17 promises that God has an opinion about the best course of action. He will reveal the exact route you should take as you wait for a child. God may direct you to cease medical intervention and wait on His timing. God may want you to pursue parenthood by taking advantage of medical technology and submitting to the advice of expert physicians. Surrender is *not* an automatic cessation of activity, but rather, an attitude of trust and submission to God's will as revealed to you for each decision.

I have put my hope in God alone to grant me a child. The doctors I see and the drugs I take seem almost secondary, although I take their advice and diligently follow each prescribed regimen. But I realize that only through God's intervention will I be given a child. Doctors and procedures do not operate independently of God's will. They cannot circumvent His plan for my life.

It's not human nature to set out on a journey without knowing the route we will take or where our trip will lead. But God asks us to move forward before He reveals all the answers. You do not have to know the entire course before you in order to set out on your journey. Just trust that each decision you make, as you put your hope and faith in God, will lead you where He means you to go. Trust that God has a course prepared for you and that He will reveal each new step before you take it.

———————

*Lord, we want to surrender to You. We want to know*
*what decisions to make as we wait for a child. We want*
*to have peace that we have done what You have asked of*

*us, and no more. As we seek wisdom for our decisions,*
*help us to know how to obey, not interfere, and how to*
*act in faith instead of reacting in fear.*

# NOTHING IS IMPOSSIBLE

*Even Elizabeth your relative is going to have a child in her old age,*
*and she who was said to be barren is in her sixth month.*
*For nothing is impossible with God.*

LUKE 1:36-37

"Nothing is impossible with God." I see the words in many places: coffee mugs, wall plaques, in popular self-help books. But did you know that God spoke these words specifically about overcoming infertility?

The book of Luke tells the story of Elizabeth, the mother of John the Baptist. By the time Elizabeth enters the scriptural picture, she's an old woman who's endured a lifetime of infertility. Despite her heartbreak, she maintains a sweet faith, choosing to believe that God is indeed good. She couldn't have known during those long, infertile years that God had chosen *her* to become the mother of a very important messenger of God's kingdom. Jesus Himself later said of her son, "Among those born of women there has not risen anyone greater than John the Baptist" (Matthew 11:11).

An angel appeared twice — once to her husband and again to Mary, the mother of Jesus — to make the announcement of John's conception and birth. God used Elizabeth's infertility as a backdrop for a miracle. He wanted to shake up a sleepy nation and prepare the people for incredible events soon to unfold.

Through this account, God lets us know in no uncertain terms that nothing, not even infertility, can thwart His purposes in our lives. *Nothing is impossible with God.* What a comfort to know these words were spoken directly into a difficult case of infertility! We can celebrate God's awesome power to move heaven and earth to accomplish His will and know that we are in the most capable hands imaginable.

And yet this can be a hard truth to celebrate. We can't understand why God would refuse to give us a child right away if He has a plan to make us parents. Perhaps the greatest challenge to our faith is accepting the mystery of God's ways and His timing. We know that He is able — praise the Lord! But while it's easy to celebrate His power, it can be hard to celebrate His timing. And yet His timing remains as critical to His plan as His power. We have to accept them both as evidence of His love for us.

---

*Lord, this is indeed the heart of the mystery of infertility:*
*to know that nothing is impossible for You, and that You*
*say You are a loving, gracious Father who loves to give us*
*good gifts — and yet You have not granted our heart's*
*desire for a child. We don't understand why You are able*
*but not willing . . . at least not yet. Perhaps in heaven*

we'll have all the answers about why we waited. But on earth, grant us more faith, and add to our faith patience and comfort!

# HOW HUSBANDS HURT

*Elkanah her husband would say to her, "Hannah, why are you weeping?*
*Why don't you eat? Why are you downhearted?*
*Don't I mean more to you than ten sons?"*

1 SAMUEL 1:8

Husbands hate to see their wives hurting. Elkanah wanted to comfort his wife, Hannah, who deeply grieved her inability to have a child. Elkanah didn't sit next to her, crying over his inability to have a child with her. Instead, he wanted to give her everything he could, to give her so much of himself that she didn't notice her barrenness.

That's the heart of a man, to insulate the woman he loves from all distress and heartache. But Elkanah couldn't protect Hannah from the grim reality of her situation. And he couldn't stop her tears.

Like Hannah, most women seem harder hit by infertility than do their husbands. Both suffer the loss, but on the surface it seems only one truly mourns — the wife. Most men do not understand how deeply rooted the dream of childbearing can be in a woman's psyche.

A friend explained how she got her husband to understand

her struggle with infertility. She asked him to imagine how he would feel if he lost his job and health and could no longer provide for her. As much as he identified his manhood with his ability to provide and protect, she said, she felt less of a woman through her inability to have a child. She knew it was wrong — and yet the pressure remained.

Men and women typically have different ways to deal with grief and pressure. Sometimes the husband can tune in better to his wife's feelings than his own. It may, therefore, seem like the delay of children doesn't mean as much to him as it does to her. Men and women process the experience of infertility differently.

Despite appearances, your husband hurts when you hurt, and he wants to comfort and protect you from the storms of life. He may also need to know how much he means to you, to feel reassured that you love him and feel happy with him even when life stinks. So give your husband the "space" he needs to grieve, when and how he needs it. Reassure him of your love and commitment and make sure he knows that your unhappiness stems from waiting for a child, not from discontent with him.

---

*Lord, show us how to love each other even when we struggle with heavy burdens. Help me today to reassure my husband of my love and commitment. Please strengthen my marriage and safeguard it from the storms raging around us. Help my husband to understand how difficult some of these issues can be for me. Help us to be* generous with our compassion for one another and to freely offer affection and reassurance when the hard times hit.

# PRAYING HUSBANDS

*Isaac prayed to the LORD on behalf of his wife, because she was barren.*
*The LORD answered his prayer, and his wife Rebekah became pregnant.*
GENESIS 25:21

What a blessed woman Rebekah was to have a husband who prayed for her! Her husband, Isaac, prayed for her because of her childlessness, and God answered his prayer by giving Rebekah a child. Isaac's prayer created an enormous blessing in their lives together and undoubtedly fostered an incredible intimacy between them.

Often it seems as if women have to carry the heavier load when dealing with infertility. Women go to most of the doctor appointments, have most of the procedures, and seem to feel the emptiness of the womb most acutely. Men often seem reduced to bystanders and can feel helpless to support and protect their wives during the crisis. Oftentimes, if a man feels helpless to change a situation, he will begin to turn his attention elsewhere, to things he can fix and control. The wife can feel abandoned and alone in their struggle to conceive. Walls begin to build, and the struggle to have a child becomes a struggle to keep the marriage together.

Husbands are not powerless, however, and in fact can have a greater impact during infertility than even the most renowned doctor or celebrated adoption director. Husbands have direct access to an all-powerful God. Men who pray for their wives provide comfort, leadership, and protection.

The husband may appear helpless to change the situation, but God is listening. A man can remind God daily of his wife's heartache and emotional needs, and ask continually for the blessing of a child. Men can carry the burden of infertility by having the strength to continually pray when the wife feels too discouraged to lift her heart back up to God.

A woman feels supernaturally comforted by a husband who prays for her. She can trust in him and take comfort in his spiritual strength and determination. The wife needs to see her husband praying with a faith that at times seems stronger than hers, and she needs to hear him as he pours out his own longings before God. Men don't have to overcome the impossible to win the hearts and respect of their wives — they have only to pray to the God who makes all things possible.

---

*Lord, You listened to Isaac's prayer for Rebekah and granted her a child because of his plea. When my husband feels powerless to help or comfort me, remind him to pray. Develop in my husband the will and strength to carry our burden to You every day, so that even in times of deep discouragement and exhaustion, I can have confidence that he is supporting and strengthening me through his prayers. As he prays for us, please listen to* and answer his prayers. Please greatly increase the intimacy of our marriage as I open my heart fully to this man who prays on my behalf during this crisis.

# PREDICTING THE FUTURE

*Diviners see visions that lie; they tell dreams that are false,*
*they give comfort in vain.*

ZECHARIAH 10:2

Have you ever felt tempted to consult a psychic to find out when or if you will have children? Ads on television, in print, and on billboards all around us bombard us with psychics who promise to tell us our future (for a small fee!). If you have a credit card, they have answers.

Sometimes the wait for God to reveal His answers seems so long and so quiet that we feel tempted to circumvent the wait by using a psychic. We thrill at the idea of having an exact date and time of when we will be blessed with a child. And the promise of having an immediate answer seems like such a relief. After all, if we at least knew how our story was going to end, the waiting wouldn't be as nerve-wracking — right? Couldn't we better serve God if we didn't feel so wrapped up in wanting to know *when*?

Maybe — but psychics don't have the answers. Zechariah 10:2 tells us that their visions do not come from God, and the "comfort" they offer is in vain. A similar warning might apply to friends and family who want to relate a dream or a "special feeling" they have about us. Very often, people will want to comfort us by making a prediction about our future — but it doesn't come from God. God doesn't warn us away from psychic predictions to spoil our fun, but to protect us from disillusionment and distress.

And as hard as it is to wait without answers, sometimes we are called to do exactly that. A Jew in World War II, trying to survive the horrors of the Nazis, anonymously penned the following poem:

> *I believe,*
> *I believe in the sun,*
> *even when it is not shining.*
> *I believe in love*
> *even when feeling it not.*
> *I believe in God*
> *even when God is silent.*

You are called to this same kind of sustaining faith. Your faith will develop and become strong as you trust in God's goodness despite His silence. Your faith will stretch as you believe in His love for you even when He denies you your heart's desire. Ask others, not for predictions, but to pray with you for the strength and courage to face the challenges ahead. And should a psychic claim to know what your future holds, remember: you already know Who holds the future.

———————

*Lord, how hard it is to wait without answers! We want an exact time and day when our prayers for a child will be answered. Not knowing makes it so hard. If we could just know the future, we believe our lives would be easier today. Please remind us that only You know our future. If we are ever tempted to listen to a psychic or someone who claims to know our future, help us to remember that only Your predictions can be trusted. Please comfort us and help us to discover the joys of trusting in You alone.*

# WATCH YOUR WORDS

*But I tell you that men will have to give account on the day of judgment*
*for every careless word they have spoken.*

MATTHEW 12:36

I had just finished an expensive month of treatments and was waiting for the dreaded pregnancy test. I showed no signs of pregnancy
and discouragement dogged my every moment. I dragged myself to
the doctor's office, and as I flopped into the chair I moaned, "I
know I'm not pregnant!"

I immediately felt a strange sense of heavenly reprimand. I
sensed that I had done something I was not supposed to, that I had
crossed some invisible line. And, indeed, I had crossed a forbidden
line: I had dishonored God by making a statement of "fact" about
the future without any regard for the Lord or His power at work in
me. I had predicted the future, engaged in a sort of fortune-telling,
so that I wouldn't feel crushed if the test came back negative.
Somehow I didn't trust God enough to allow the moment to
unfold as He had ordained it. I didn't trust that God would keep
me from feeling crushed beyond all repair by a negative result.

You can't tell if you're pregnant just from signs and symptoms.
Your body can play all sorts of tricks on an anxious mind. Women

waiting to become pregnant can read a great deal of fantasy into the reality of each little twinge and sensation. The pregnancy test becomes almost a formality, because her mind gets made up long before taking the test.

Waiting to test, in fact, usually becomes a time of overwhelming obsession. Because so much hangs in the balance, everything we experience and feel becomes a possible indicator of our future. Will we be parents at last? Or will we be sentenced to another month of waiting? Is that burning sensation I feel today in my abdomen the lunch I just ate — or a pregnancy implanting in my womb?

You and I don't know the future, not even ten minutes from now. You don't know how your body works in secret or when or if you'll conceive. It is not our place to make predictions or to voice our opinions about the unknown future as facts. The future belongs to God alone, and only He knows if we're pregnant (or will be soon). We may have a "special feeling" about this month's cycle or we may become convinced God will not answer our prayers at all. Whatever we "feel," it is important that we express these stirrings as opinions and not fact.

God's Word tells us that some day we will have to answer for every careless word we've spoken, including offhanded predictions about pregnancy. God does not treat words lightly! Making predictions about what we don't know trespasses into God's exclusive territory.

———

*Lord, when emotions run high it becomes easy to say*
*things we don't mean. Our words have an impact on our*

*lives that we don't fully understand, and we are only now beginning to see how carefully You listen to each word we speak. Help us to look to You for reassurance about our future so that we do not feel tempted to make predictions or statements on our own. Guard our hearts, thoughts, and mouths!*

# STORMS OF EMOTION

*In bitterness of soul Hannah wept much and prayed to the LORD.*

1 SAMUEL 1:10

How do you think a spiritual person should handle her emotions? Do you picture someone sitting serenely, never raising her voice or shaking an angry fist? The story of Hannah gives us a refreshing glimpse of a godly woman handling a natural emotion.

Hannah suffered a long time with barrenness and felt "deeply troubled" both by her situation and by God's seeming refusal to grant her a child. As she prayed to the Lord about her infertility, she described her "misery" and "great anguish and grief." A nearby priest saw her praying and mistook her anguish for drunkenness.

The remarkable thing about Hannah's faith is not only her honesty regarding her hurt and bitterness, but her ability to pray right in the middle of it. Raging emotions can make us feel separated from God, too sorrowful or angry to pray. Our emotions seem to push God away. Reading the Bible can feel impossible — nothing seems to make sense and our eyes can't focus on the page. Is He able to pull us toward Him through the haze of disillusionment? It seems impossible. Instead it appears likely that our faith will collapse and we'll lose the battle, for how could God overcome our powerful emotions?

Have you ever felt that, as a Christian, God expects you to handle pain and adversity with a smile on your face, with never a complaint about your distress? Well, thankfully, God wants us to express everything to Him, as openly and honestly as Hannah did. You may think it seems disrespectful or wrong to express bitterness over your situation to the One who has allowed it, but Hannah didn't. And don't forget, God answered her prayers with the birth of her first, Samuel, and later several other children.

Expressing your emotions, even the "negative" ones, will never cause God to withhold His blessings from you. Somehow, we have latched on to the idea that our emotions — like sadness, longing, and grief — make God angry and that we have to get rid of them before facing Him. But God knows the depth of your sorrow and He wants you to pour out your heart to Him. You have complete freedom to express your emotions — and expect to find comfort and understanding in return.

Faith does not require us to shelve our emotions during adversity. Faith supplies us with the courage to withstand the strongest storms of emotion, still believing that God loves us even when we feel unloved and unlovable.

---

*Lord, sometimes I feel overrun with strong emotions. I
wonder if you're disappointed in me when I get so afraid
or angry and frustrated. Please give me such confidence*

*in Your love for me that I know I can open my heart
before You and find an embrace of understanding and
comfort.*

# SOMEWHERE BETWEEN UTOPIA AND RUIN

*Jesus looked at them and said,*
*"With man this is impossible, but with God all things are possible."*

MATTHEW 19:26

When you guess at what the future may hold for you, do you imagine possibilities that frighten you? Do you feel certain that you could never be happy if God allowed you to remain childless? Do you fear that you will not feel satisfied if you adopt? Do you wonder if you'll feel cheated or abnormal if you have to resort to fertility treatments?

Each of us has in our minds and hearts a happy ending for our story of struggle. You may envision twins, a double blessing for your heartache. Or you may envision a surprise pregnancy after all medical efforts have failed. You want to hold on to your dream of a child and living happily ever after.

The alternatives scare us to death — the other unwritten endings that plague us in our nightmares, or when our hearts grow fatigued from the battle. We may have shadowy visions of a bleak life without children or of adoptions that end in disaster. It seems as if our hopes swing wildly somewhere between utopia and ruin.

God, the author of our story, does not want us to imagine the ending in merely human terms. You are not playing a game in which the only alternatives are despair or contentment. The miracle you can expect is that no matter how your story ends, it *will be* a happy one. God can make any situation into a life of abundant blessings and joy.

At the cross, Christ banished your worst fears about infertility. There exists no situation and no set of circumstances that prevent God from blessing you. God promises to enable you to feel peace, hope, and joy. You can take those nightmares that plague you, those unanswered dreams and an empty heart, and lay them at Jesus' feet. It may seem impossible to you right now to believe that you will be happy no matter how God chooses to answer your prayers, but it is true — with God all things are possible!

———————

*Lord, sometimes I feel I will be happy only if You answer my prayers exactly as I specify. Thank you for expanding my horizons to include the unlimited possibility of You. Thank you for Your incredible promise that all things are possible with You. I still want my prayers answered according to my heart's desire for children — but now I know that I don't need to be afraid if your plan differs from mine. Thank you for the endings I've never thought of, and thank you for rescuing me from black-and-white thinking. Just as I can't fully understand* what You are doing in my life today, I cannot fully understand what You plan to do tomorrow.

# CHRISTMAS IS FOR . . . .

*But the angel said to them, "Do not be afraid. I bring you good news of great joy
that will be for all the people. Today in the town of David
a Savior has been born to you; he is Christ the Lord."*

LUKE 2:10-11

Have you ever heard the expression, "Christmas is for children?" I
know it's the Yuletide season when I begin to see nightly reruns of
favorite holiday cartoons and hear news reports of parents standing in line all night outside a store to make sure they get the hot
new toy every kid wants.

Yet Christmas can be a lonely time to be childless. Hanging
only two stockings by the fireplace can dishearten you when you've
always imagined hanging several in a row. Even the Nativity scene
can upset you with its picture of an infant and an overjoyed family
and admirers.

Some seasons I have felt almost silly, or even secretly ashamed,
to celebrate the season with "just" my husband. But can you name
the first Christmas present and to whom it was given? Luke 2:10-
11 records the angelic announcement that God has given a gift to
"all the world."

The angel announced that God intended Jesus' birth as a miracle, personally, for *you*. Jesus Christ, our Savior "has been born unto *you*." Even as you long for a child to fill your home, God intended this birth to fill your heart. God fully intends that you celebrate the season as much as any child or any family with children.

During this holiday season, you can rejoice in the knowledge that God already has blessed you through the birth of Jesus. You can continue to hope for the birth of a child into your family, even as you celebrate the birth of Christ into the world.

Since God refuses to exclude you from the festivities, perhaps you can find a way to share His joy with someone else who feels left out. How can you share the blessing of this Christmas birth God has given you? Ask God to lead you to someone or some organization that needs to experience the Great Joy of Christmas.

Christmas is indeed for everyone: adults, children, poor and rich, all nationalities, and walks of life. Carry the angel's words with you everywhere this season. "Do not be afraid! There is good news of great joy, meant for you! A Savior has been born to you!"

---

*Lord, the news is good, and the joy of Christ is great!
Please help me to celebrate this birth as a personal gift
from You, even as I long for the birth of my own child.
Help me to spread good news and great joy wherever I
go. Thank you that when loneliness and sadness threaten
to steal the blessings of the season, I can remember that
this heavenly birth was for me, from You. Help me to
share in the great joy of Christ's birth, a birth that did*

*not isolate me from others but brought me into a family of believers. And please show us how to share this blessing with others. Merry Christmas, Lord!*

# WONDERING, NOT WANDERING

*All the days ordained for me were written in your book*
*before one of them came to be.*

PSALM 139:16

The Bible says that God knows the exact number of days in our lives and that He plans each day for us before we are born. He knows us intimately, long before our mothers were born or felt the first twinge of pregnancy. We see the linear progression of our lives. God sees the eternal past and future and knows how all of the events we face will fit together to accomplish His will.

Only God knows why your waiting to conceive is a necessary, critical part of His plan.

Because we can't see our situation through God's eternal perspective, we feel tempted to slide toward generalities. We simply want a child. We don't know what might lie in the balance of when we conceive and which child we are given, so we think we could get any child at any time in order to be fulfilled.

But right at this moment God is orchestrating so much more than your life. His care and control over the events of the world do not diminish in the slightest His care for you. Rather, He is moving the world together for the perfect time for each child to be born.

The Bible insists there is an ordained day for every baby to be born, and so it follows that there is an ordained day for every baby to be conceived. If you are waiting to become pregnant, you have the assurance of knowing that God is not putting you off or ignoring your request or wasting time. If God has chosen to grant you children, He is even now moving you toward an exact day and time for you, or a birth mother, to conceive, and an exact day for this sweet baby to be born. It is hard to understand why we must wait for this appointed day when we feel we would be happy with *any* baby we could conceive between now and then. And it can confuse us to know whether or how we should pursue medical treatment, since God already has pre-ordained everything.

But we know only part of His plan for our lives; He reveals to us daily how we are to live in each moment. We are asked to entrust the whole of our lives — including this struggle — to Him. Because we know He plans each birth and life so carefully, we can take comfort in the knowledge that He is a God of specifics. We may be *wondering* about the road we're on, but we're not *wandering* on an aimless path. It may seem that time waiting is time wasted, but in truth, each day that passes brings us closer to the specific day that God may have appointed for our child to be born.

---

*Lord, we know only part of Your plan and yet You ask us to trust You completely. We want to know how many days of waiting we'll face, and You ask us to remain content with Your plan for today. This waiting doesn't make sense to us and we need reassurance of Your love for us and Your complete and masterful control over this situation. We want a baby so dearly! Please show us today how You appoint a time and season to everyone and everything. Help us take comfort in the knowledge that You may be preparing us for a very specific date ahead when we will finally hold our child, the specific child You have ordained for us to rear.*

# AN APPOINTED TIME
# FOR BLESSINGS

*And now you will be silent and not able to speak until the day this happens,*
*because you did not believe my words,* which will come true at their
proper time. . . .When his time of service was completed, *he*
*returned home. After this his wife Elizabeth became pregnant.*

LUKE 1:20-24 (EMPHASIS ADDED)

Two thousand years after his death, we remember John the Baptist
as a great prophet and minister who prepared his countrymen for
the arrival of Jesus. He also shared a unique trait with several other
major Bible figures: he was born to a formerly infertile mother.

Luke tells us that an angel appeared to a priest named
Zechariah to tell him that his barren, elderly wife would have a son.
Zechariah, then serving his shift in the temple, replied in disbelief:
"How can I be sure of this?" (Luke 1:18). After all, he and his wife
had long since passed childbearing age and had remained infertile
throughout their marriage. Long ago they had abandoned all hope
of having a baby. The angel, irritated at the man's impudence,
struck Zechariah mute until the infant arrived.

I find it especially interesting that Zechariah still had to finish
out his duty in the temple before returning home. God announced

His intention to miraculously bless Zechariah and Elizabeth with a child — a prophet who would shake history — but they still had to wait to conceive. Their plight defies human logic.

We tend to think that if God wanted to bring a great person into the world, He'd snap His fingers and cause it to happen immediately. But instead, when the angel announced God's intentions, the formerly infertile couple still had to pass some time before they could become pregnant.

The story of Zechariah and Elizabeth reminds me that God's blessings are not haphazard. Each one has an appointed, proper time. And although waiting may feel counter-productive to God's purposes, it remains a part of His plan.

---

*Lord, how we wish for an angel to announce Your plan to us! But even if one did, we don't know how we would feel about waiting for the "proper" time for Your blessing. We want Your blessing — but we also want it right now! Thank you that you are a God of details, carefully selecting a proper time for Your miracles. Please help us to continue serving You joyfully as we wait for Your timing. Thank you, too, for giving us so many reminders throughout the Bible that You can intervene and overcome infertility at any moment.*

# IS GOD MAD AT ME?

*The LORD, the LORD, the compassionate and gracious God, slow to anger,*
*abounding in love and faithfulness, maintaining love to thousands, and forgiving*
*wickedness, rebellion and sin.*

EXODUS 34:6-7

Is God punishing you with infertility because of your sins? Perhaps
you had an abortion, were promiscuous, or rebelled against God.
Can there be any hope for you?

It is true that infertility *can* be a consequence of sin.
Reproductive systems scarred from abortions or by diseases trans-
mitted through sexually illicit behavior may close a woman's womb.
God encourages obedience to biblical principles precisely because
He wants us to avoid that kind of suffering, not because He wants
to inflict pain on us.

Much to the contrary, God describes Himself as a loving, gracious, compassionate heavenly Father. He does not easily get angry
but remains eager to forgive you and draw you close. God does not
rejoice to see you suffer, even if the suffering can be traced to
ungodly behavior.

But still you may wonder: *Is God mad at me for some unconfessed sin?*
Or perhaps you are not a Christian yet and fear you can't come to

God because of your past. Listen — God promises each of us that if we will accept Jesus Christ, His Son, as our Savior and ask Him to live in our hearts and direct our paths, He will forgive us our sins. He will make us "new creations," removing forever everything old, including our sins and mistakes.

With God so ready to offer His forgiveness and compassion, you do not need to fear that He is punishing you with infertility. If past sins haunt you, perhaps you need to tell God about them and receive His forgiveness. Please let your mind be at rest, knowing that God loves you and is not angry with you. No matter the reason for your struggle to conceive a child, God will be gracious to you. He eagerly extends His mercy and tender forgiveness whenever you ask — and especially when you feel unworthy. As the apostle John wrote, because of God's grace, "we set our hearts at rest in his presence whenever our hearts condemn us. For God is greater than our hearts, and he knows everything" (1 John 3:19-20).

----

*Lord, thank you that this struggle has caused me to turn to You for answers and help. But sometimes, God, You seem so far away — and when answers and help don't seem to come, I begin to wonder if You're mad at me. When I have these moments, please remind me of these verses. If physical consequences from past sins haunt me, please help me to be free of remorse as I trust in You to guide my life in moving forward. You are such a powerful God — please let me see Your tender side as I reveal my failures. I know that because I love Jesus and He is my Savior, You have forgiven me completely!*

## COMFORTING OTHERS

*Do not let your hearts be troubled. Trust in God; trust also in me.*
*In my Father's house there are many rooms; if it were not so,*
*I would have told you. I am going there to prepare a place for you.*

JOHN 14:1-2

Just the other day, my friend Kimberly did the most extraordinary thing. A close friend had suffered a miscarriage, and Kimberly didn't know what to say to comfort her. Because Kimberly knew I had endured my own miscarriages, she called for help. She rattled off everything she wanted to say and asked me to point out anything that might unintentionally hurt or seem insensitive.

I felt amazed at Kimberly's compassion for her friend. If only everyone (including me!) were that sensitive when we tried to comfort others who suffer!

After I suffered a miscarriage or another failed cycle of trying to conceive, some people would try to comfort me, only to hurt me with insensitive remarks. As we chatted over coffee, one friend commented rather lightheartedly, "Well, it wasn't God's will for this baby to live." Sometimes people avoided me because they just didn't know what to say. Suffering makes people uncomfortable, and they're either going to say everything that comes to mind or nothing at all. People feel so awkward around us that *we* end up comforting *them*!

If you want to hold onto these friendships, you must learn to help your friends work through their discomfort. It's not fair that the injured party has to heal someone else, but there it is. We have to help our friends and family know what to say and what can be done to help us. Although it may feel like an unjust burden, it can actually furnish an opportunity to teach others about what comforts you the most and how they can reach out to you when you're hurting. You may be suffering, but you have to help the people around you to feel comfortable with your pain.

One day shortly before His execution, Jesus spoke to His disciples about the heaven awaiting them and encouraged them not to feel troubled by the events about to unfold. Although Jesus was the one about to suffer, He spent His last free moments comforting those closest to Him. Jesus knew His disciples would watch Him suffer, but He didn't want them to feel overwhelmed to the point of despair.

Your suffering, like that of Jesus, can create a multitude of blessings. Relationships can become sweetly intimate when friends see your vulnerability and discover what speaks to your heart. As these friends learn through you how to respond to pain with compassion and tact, they become well-equipped to comfort others.

---

*Lord, just as You comforted those around You when You*
*suffered, so help me to be sensitive to the people around*
*me. Some people feel so uncomfortable with suffering*

and with delayed hopes and prayers! I am in a unique
position to guide them out of hurting into helpfulness.
Grant me compassion toward their awkwardness and the
joy of following your example in comforting others. May
my suffering produce a rich yield of blessings for
generations to come.

# WISDOM FOR MEDICAL DECISIONS

*If any of you lacks wisdom, he should ask God,*
*who gives generously to all without finding fault.*

JAMES 1:5

What doctors can do these days with a sperm and an egg—
incredible! Even more startling are medical advances in genetics.
But precisely because of all the new procedures, couples may feel
bombarded by choices, each of which can present a spiritual,
physical and emotional tangle to sort out.

In all our choices, we can count on and expect God to direct us
in a holy manner as we seek to please Him. Some of the procedures
are so new that it can be difficult to understand all their implica-
tions; fear may creep in that God will become angry if we acciden-
tally make a bad choice. But we have an antidote to this fear, just as
surely as a dawn follows every night.

Learn everything you can about each procedure you are
considering. If your doctor is not a Christian, ask for a referral to a
Christian physician familiar with these procedures so that you can
ask for a spiritual opinion. And most importantly, pray about *every-*
*thing.* Ask a few faithful friends to pray with you for wisdom, then

give yourself plenty of time to make each decision. God promises to guide us through each individual decision, no matter how small or how large. We can rest assured that if God is directing our path, we will steer clear of the pitfalls.

If you have a particularly troublesome or large decision to make, you can also devote extended periods of time to pray over your decision. Close the door to your bedroom and set aside an hour with your spouse to kneel and ask for wisdom. Don't be surprised if nothing obvious happens while you are praying, or if neither one of you has any better idea what to do when you're done. Trust that your prayers were heard and then wait to see the answer reveal itself.

During my own struggle with infertility, I faced an enormous decision. I needed an operation performed by only four doctors in the world — and I had to choose between two doctors. Both seemed extremely qualified, but I strongly preferred the doctor who had less experience with the surgery. I prayed constantly about my decision but felt so stressed that "hearing" God seemed virtually impossible. So I tried something I had never done: I fasted. Fasting means you do not eat, but do drink liquids, for an entire day. You try to lessen distractions around you in order to become more attuned to the Holy Spirit.

I did not receive any clear answers during that day — a disappointment — but I did feel more peaceful and calm as I thought about the crisis. Late that night, however, I woke up to hear myself praying aloud — and telling God which surgeon I would choose! The answer came while I slept . . . and God greatly blessed the decision.

However you pursue God's perfect wisdom, He promises to bless you. He does not wait for you to make a mistake so He can punish you. God wants to reveal the answer and bless you for seeking Him.

----

*Lord, I lay everything at Your feet: my desire for a child, my fear of making a wrong choice, and my deep desire to see You honored and glorified, however You may choose to answer my prayer. I claim James 1:5 now, and know that because I ask for wisdom, You will give it, and give generously. Thank you for opening my eyes and heart to Your gentle, loving direction!*

# THE LONGEST STRETCH OF TIME

*For he has not despised or disdained the suffering of the afflicted one;*
*he has not hidden his face from him but has listened to his cry for help.*

PSALM 22:24

Occasionally on the news I hear of people stranded for days at sea, on mountains, or in the snow, who wait for anyone to see and rescue them. Can you imagine their joy and relief when a rescue plane finally circles overhead? They had feared for their lives. They assumed they would die in their distress — but at last they knew their cries had been heard.

Ironically, many survivors will tell you that the hardest part of their ordeal occurred while waiting those final few hours. The longest stretch of time occurred between knowing they'd been heard and waiting for the final moment of rescue.

Psalm 22 promises victims of infertility that our cries have been heard. We are not so lost that God cannot find us, nor so isolated that He can't rescue us. Time may seem to stand still as we wait, knowing our prayers have been heard, and yet still waiting for the final moment of release.

Somehow, knowing that God has heard our cries can make it harder to keep praying when no answer seems to come. We begin to doubt ourselves, and then Him. If God is listening to our cries, if He truly cares about our suffering, then why hasn't He intervened? Long-time Christians often emphasize that God can choose two ways to rescue us: He can rescue out of the situation, or He can deliver us from the emotions that rage within us.

But no matter how He rescues you, He wants to assure you that He does not despise or disdain your suffering. He knows how hard it is for you to wait. He is not hiding His face, but is making Himself available to you at every moment. I know there is an agony in knowing He is so close and yet has not rescued you. Why not? I don't know. All I can say with certainty is that God's message to you is simply, *your suffering matters.*

---

*Lord, thank you for hearing my prayers. I know my rescue is close at hand. I am not sure how You'll save me in this situation. You may choose to calm the storming emotions but leave me in this stranded boat. You may choose to move me entirely out of this situation by granting me a pregnancy or adoption. The emotions of what I've been through, and the emotions of my hopes and dreams, can be so hard to manage as I wait these final moments to see Your rescue take place. I know I was safe the moment my cries reached Your ears, but I long to see Your rescue taking place. Please come quickly!*

# HOPE IS STRONGER THAN FEAR

*Weeping may remain for a night, but rejoicing comes in the morning.*

PSALM 30:5

When a close friend suffered through repeated miscarriages and yet found the strength to try to conceive once more, I felt astounded. How did she find the strength, I wondered, to continue to reach for happiness, knowing such great pain might ensue? She thought for a moment and replied, "Because hope ultimately is stronger than fear."

She was right. That's why Psalm 30:5 reminds us that rejoicing will eventually overtake all tears. God graciously gives us a clear picture of the role both weeping and rejoicing will play in our lives. God acknowledges that we will weep, and at times our lives will seem as dark as a night without stars. But God also promises us that our grief will not last forever. Our birthright as His children is joy. Circumstances may make us temporarily unhappy, but knowing we are sustained by a wildly loving, overwhelmingly powerful God brings us joy, no matter what we face. When weeping and grief seem to overshadow this reality, God assures us that these feelings will pass as surely as night gives way to morning.

We all want to know that the grief we feel as we wait for children will turn to joy when God finally blesses us with a child. But heaven's promise of joy does not depend on circumstances. God promises that we will rejoice regardless of how He answers our prayers. Your greatest fear may be never having children. God asks that you trust Him and know that you will be able to rejoice even if *that* should come to pass.

God works unexpected miracles in unanticipated ways. He assures you of a happy ending, of overflowing joy in your life no matter how He chooses to answer your requests.

---

*Lord, thank you for promising that this trial will end*
*someday, because at times I can't imagine continuing*
*with the heavy burden of grief. Thank you for assuring*
*me that I will rejoice with You again. I need these*
*glimpses of victory as I fight the battle of faith.*

# THE MEANING OF SURRENDER

*"For I know the plans I have for you," declares the* LORD, *"plans to prosper you and not to harm you, plans to give you hope and a future."*

JEREMIAH 29:11

A woman on a popular radio talk show was describing her secret for getting what she wanted out of God and life: "The moment I surrender it and give it up," she explained, "that's when it comes to pass."

Perhaps it had worked exactly that way in one moment of her life, but no one seemed to question why she still obviously struggled in many other areas of living. If surrender provided the unfailing key to unlock all blessings, why hadn't she just surrendered all her other problems as well?

You, too, may hear stories from well-meaning acquaintances who declare that once they surrendered, they got their answer. They encourage you to surrender your desire to have a child in order to expedite God's blessing. The false belief is that if we can muster up enough of this feeling of surrender, if we can somehow cast aside this burning desire for a child, then God will finally act on our behalf. This assumes that God frowns on desires and longings — but no one can ever satisfactorily explain how to cast aside these intense feelings or why strong feelings so upset God. If this myth of surrender were true, wouldn't that reduce God to little more than a mathematical equation or a robot that automatically responds to the right coded sequence? If surrender equals success, this would mean that the power to answer our prayers lies in our hands, not God's. God would become little more than a middleman, raising or lowering the gate to our blessings when we enter the right password.

A weathered old man once described to me his understanding of surrender. He said that he had a mean, grisly cat that wasn't afraid to use its claws and teeth. Every once in a while, the cat would get into some mischief outdoors and need a good bath. My friend would fill up the kitchen sink with warm, sudsy water, grab the cat, and dunk him in. The cat would hiss and claw and refuse to surrender to the bath. But the cat's reaction really didn't matter, because it would get a bath either way. I am inclined to believe that we are in a similar situation as we wait for a child: we can either hiss and claw or surrender, but the outcome will remain the same regardless.

We don't have to rid ourselves of natural, God-given desires before God will act on our behalf. Surrender isn't some magical key to unlock God's heart. God has plans to bless us, and He will not withhold this blessing even if we never get a complete grip on all of the emotions that burst within us.

---

*Lord, when it seems we get no answer to our prayers, we*
*feel tempted to believe that we lack something inside us.*
*We think that if we just tried harder or had more faith,*

You would deliver us. Help us understand what surrender means in our specific situation. Give us the peace to know that it's okay to want a child fiercely and that our stormy emotions won't sway You off course.

# WAITING *IS* THE ANSWER

*Shall we accept good from God, and not trouble?*
JOB 2:10

Infertility is defined by waiting: waiting for your period to start; waiting for ovulation; waiting for medications to take effect; waiting for insurance coverage to begin; waiting for test results; waiting for advice as to which tests to do next.

I reached a point in my struggle with infertility when doctors told me, at last, the wait was over. I had been marvelously, miraculously cured from a physical defect of my reproductive system. After one final surgery in January, I remember waking from the anesthesia to hear my doctor pronounce me ready. "Go out and have children!" he laughed, adding that there no longer existed any obvious reason why I couldn't.

I can't tell you how thrilled I felt that my wait was ending. I can tell you that I went home and promptly, triumphantly, inhaled a box of chocolates. (My post-operative directions said to start off eating semi-soft foods, and cherry cordials did have a moist center!) I danced around my living room and rang up an exorbitant long-distance bill to tell my family and friends that, at last, I was on my way to motherhood.

But I didn't get pregnant in January. Or in February. Or even that spring or summer. The waiting that I had so gladly bid adieu once again made itself my unwelcome companion. No explanation came, either medical or spiritual. I had to make peace with a lack of reasons for my wait.

God used that time to show me that waiting is not counter-productive. Waiting is not an unanswered prayer. Waiting *is* the answer. For reasons known only to God, you, too, must wait for a child right now.

But do not think this is some second-best, unexpected plan for your life. This is God's anticipated best plan for your future. Waiting is no mere interruption or a nasty wrench in the works. God uses waiting as an active tool in His hands as He shapes our destiny — even if we don't seem well-equipped to enjoy it!

I have never known anyone desperately longing for a dream to be fulfilled who enjoyed waiting for it. Everything in us screams to take control and get what we want; it seems against the very grain of our nature to wait. Waiting seems *wrong*. No best-selling books teach us how to master the art of waiting; even the experts have to grit their teeth and endure it. No one wants to study it, read about it, or (much less) experience it.

And yet we wait.

---

*Lord, please change the way we see waiting. Help us to see that it is not our enemy, but a part of Your wonder-ful, divine plan for us. Teach us to look for its hidden*

treasures and to conquer our feelings of doubt and
impatience. Help us to look back on our waiting with
fond memories as we recall how You led us
through this difficult time.

# THE QUESTION WHY

*Now we see but a poor reflection as in a mirror; then we shall see face to face.*
*Now I know in part; then I shall know fully, even as I am fully known.*
*And now these three remain: faith, hope and love.*

I CORINTHIANS 13:12-13

I had a friend in high school named Lacy. Like me, Lacy followed Christ. Unlike me, Lacy was the homecoming queen and head cheerleader. She always smiled and said "hi" to me when we passed in the halls, no matter how my popularity fared on any given day. She knew my name and always seemed interested in my activities — small acts of friendship, to be sure, but in those turbulent years, they meant a great deal.

Sadly, Lacy's mother died, breaking her heart and the heart of her father. And then, unthinkably, Lacy also died. Now, many years later, I still don't understand why she had to die so young. And I can't begin to imagine the anguish her father felt, and perhaps feels even today. By now, I am sure Lacy's possessions have all been boxed up and given away. There seems little physical evidence that she ever existed.

But I Corinthians warns us not to peer too closely at the surface of such events if we want to see the real answer. In fact, God tells us that we see only "a poor reflection" of life. God promises that when we see Him face-to-face in heaven, we will understand the "why" of our lives. C. S. Lewis describes that moment: "The bad dream will be over: it will be morning."[1]

On earth, our questions often go unanswered. But while we still dream on earth, God has told us how we are to live: by faith, hope, and love. By faith, believing that God loves us and is at work in our situation, even when all evidence seems contrary. By hope, believing God can work unexpected miracles at unlikely times and that He has a plan for our redemption. And by love, reaching out to others to share the contentment we have found in Christ even as we wait.

God promises that although many of our questions must go unanswered for today, these three comforts will sustain us until we finally see Him face-to-face.

---

*Lord, circumstances can be so cruel; to know the answer "why" seems absolutely critical. It feels like the only evidence confirming You as a good and capable God. You know how important the question "why" is to us, and You promise to answer it . . . someday. Thank you for showing us how to live with the question still unanswered. Help us today to continue by faith, hope and Your love.*

# IT SEEMS SO UNFAIR

*God does not judge by external appearance.*

GALATIANS 2:6

Do you ever envy pregnant women, perhaps even resent them? Does your heart especially break with resentment and confusion when you see an unmarried, pregnant teenager, or a woman who can't stay off drugs and yet repeatedly conceives?

It doesn't make any sense to us why God allows these women, who seem so unfit for motherhood and so far away from God, to conceive, while we serve and love Him and yet remain childless. But God sees what we do not, and His desire to touch the lives of these women defies our comprehension.

If we judged by appearances, it would seem that life and God are both unfair. Although we put God on trial in our hearts, He doesn't seem to provide much of a defense. Because He doesn't seem present, we go on and convict Him, pronouncing our sentence: *Incapable. Cold. Indifferent. Spiteful.* Bitterness seeps through our souls, hardening us to God's message of grace and mercy. *After all, we reason, if God allows such injustice, how can we trust Him?*

A teenaged mother recently recounted how difficult it was to be a young, unmarried mom. She knew she had made mistakes but was determined to make things right for herself and her child. She needed support and encouragement to stay on the right track. She needed forgiveness. Sadly, the one place she felt most uncomfortable was church. The condescending glares she received from other women made her feel ashamed and unable to ask for help.

If we pass judgment on the appearance of another woman's life, we may miss the chance to see God do something extraordinary in her heart . . . and in ours. The women who glared at the young mom missed an opportunity to witness the incredible, redemptive power of God.

You might well be a better parent than those women you see on the street and in the news, but that does not permit you to believe they are unworthy of redemption and love. Pray for their healing and salvation. Pray for a forgiving spirit that seeks to understand their pain instead of judging their mistakes. Instead of begrudging them their child, pray for that little one.

---

*Lord, it seems so unfair that You grant people children who don't appear to deserve them. Thank you that we don't have to judge life situations by their appearance. Thank you for showing us there is always more than meets the eye, because You are at work in the world around us. Catch us before we pass judgment on another woman, and help us instead to bless her and pray for her and her child.*

# PUNISHMENT OR PREPARATION?

*"Neither this man nor his parents sinned," said Jesus, " but this happened so that the work of God might be displayed in his life."*

JOHN 9:3

The book of John tells how Jesus healed a blind man. The town's religious leaders asked why the blind man had suffered such a terrible affliction. They assumed it had to result from sin. Jesus set them straight and His answer should give you great hope and peace.

No one's sin had caused the blindness, Jesus explained, "but this happened so that the work of God might be displayed in his life." The blindness occurred, not as a punishment, but so that God might display His awesome power and love. What the religious leaders saw as a curse, God meant as an undeniable affirmation of His love and care.

Waiting for a child can be a lonely, silent time. Our minds try to find the answer to the question of "why." Sometimes we decide — or others tell us! — that God has allowed this difficulty because we have sinned. During my wait for a child, a guest once left a pamphlet behind in plain view in my kitchen. The tract proclaimed that if prayers go unanswered, the fault can always be traced to hidden, unconfessed sin. I know this friend was trying to be helpful, but I couldn't help feeling accused and judged. Was my trial really the result of sin? Or was God up to something incredible? First Peter 1:6-7 encouraged me that although

> . . . *now for a little while you may have had to suffer grief in all kinds of trials. These have come so that your faith — of greater worth than gold, which perishes even though refined by fire — may be proved genuine and may result in praise, glory and honor when Jesus Christ is revealed.*

Infertility is just one of many trials you face, and will face. God is not punishing you, but preparing you. There is much more at stake today than whether God will grant you a child. God is setting the stage for an incredible display of His power in your life. God is also refining your faith so that you will receive "praise, glory and honor" when Christ returns.

I hope that on Judgment Day, I get seated right next to my pamphlet-dropping friend. Won't she be surprised!

———————

*Lord, when we look for answers, protect us from being misled. What we see as an affliction, You may see as the preface to an incredible miracle. Reveal to us Your incredible love for us in this specific situation. We know that this has happened so that Your work will be displayed in our lives. Thank you!*

# LAUGHING OUT LOUD

*A cheerful heart is good medicine.*

PROVERBS 17:22

It can be difficult to remain cheerful while struggling with an unre-
solved crisis. It might seem phony to laugh or smile at those around
you. What could possibly make us laugh or smile, after all? Barbara
Johnson, in her book, *Leaking Laffs Between Pampers and Depends*, writes:

> No, it's not always easy being a joyful woman. Most of us are more
> experienced in grumbling than glowing. But to those who've learned
> to "count it all joy," the boomerang blessings far outnumber the
> bruises. When you feel as if you're wandering aimlessly in the wilder-
> ness of some grief-filled desert, look around you — and find the
> manna for joy that God has provided. Life isn't always what we want,
> but it's what we've got. So, with God's help, choose to be joyful.[2]

What makes you laugh out loud and feel good? Because I love
animals, we bought a Saint Bernard puppy. He went from ten
pounds to close to two hundred in just over a year. During his
growth spurts he grew a quarter-pound every eight hours! We lost

two Thanksgiving turkeys, the carpet in the family room, and most of our shoes to his wild, puppy ways. But we loved every minute of it and his presence lifted much of the gloom out of our home and hearts.

That's your mission today — to look for and find what God has given you to laugh at and smile over. The Great Physician has prescribed laughter and cheer to refresh you for the moment. We might have to wait, but we don't have to suffer.

----

*Lord, thank you for therapeutic laughter and good cheer!*
*Tickle my funny bone today. Put people in my path who*
*are contagiously cheerful. Remind me of what's ridiculous*
*in my life. And help me to share my laughter and cheer*
*with someone who needs it as much, if not more, than I do.*

# HONESTY WITH GOD

*I will show you what he is like who comes to me and hears my words and puts them into practice. He is like a man building a house, who dug down deep and laid the foundation on rock. When a flood came, the torrent struck that house but could not shake it, because it was well built. But the one who hears my words and does not put them into practice is like a man who built a house on the ground without a foundation. The moment the torrent struck that house, it collapsed and its destruction was complete.*

LUKE 6:47-49

For years, when I read Jesus' story about wise and foolish builders, I assumed that storms would always come from the outside. Life has taught me, however, that internal storms can cause just as much havoc as those that beat against my windows.

The storms that darken our skies and rush toward us most often come from within. Bitter emotions boil up and threaten to overpower us. Sorrow and longing rise until they break the dam of our mental reserves. Either we will find the strength to withstand the torrent, or it will sweep us away.

Which builder, and which house, will survive? Each decision we make and every action we take lays a brick in our lives — either we act in the faith and knowledge of Jesus Christ, or we don't. If you have built your life on Jesus Christ, your work will survive. If you don't have Christ, you cannot understand and apply His word. We will build with what we have — and apart from God, our resources soon run out. Without God, we cannot lay a solid foundation. So which do we choose? Jesus' story warns us that we have a direct hand in whether we survive life's storms.

Faith does not mean the absence of negative emotions, but the assurance that God will listen to our bitter cries as readily as He hears our prayers of thanksgiving. My mother often says, "You can feel whatever you want, just as long as you tell God about it." Emotions, no matter how strong and bitter, can never separate you from the love of God. Pour out your pain and anger to God as freely as you express gratitude — and trust Him to sort through the mess.

---

*Lord, sometimes we feel anger and disillusionment, rage and hopelessness. It feels wrong to express all these to You, especially when we may be feeling some of those bitter emotions about You and Your timing! Please give us a peaceful reassurance that we have a safe harbor in You, where we can weather the storms of emotion and then rest quietly in Your arms.*

# FINDING COURAGE

*Be strong and courageous. Do not be afraid or discouraged . . .*
*for there is a greater power with us.*

2 CHRONICLES 32:7

I love a good scare. In fact, when my husband travels, I rent every scary movie I can find and stay up late into the night, alternately terrorizing and then comforting myself with ice cream and forcing my dog to inspect every closet. Even though I understand rationally that the events on the screen have nothing to do with me and no impact on my life, my heart still pounds and my mind continues to race. I find it hard to separate fact from fiction when I dwell on something frightening.

I have pretty much the same reaction when watching the evening news. I see stories reporting statistics on the astronomical difficulty of conception after a certain age, and I panic. Then I happen to catch an exposé covering the "hidden" risks of fertility treatments. They may predict increased health risks for women who never become pregnant, or they may feature stories of failed adoptions. In those moments, wanting to have a child can seem as foolish as thinking the deranged psycho onscreen will die before the next sequel. I begin to dwell on the frightening possibilities lurking everywhere, and I just can't settle my mind.

Does it seem to you that although we lack any sweet certainties in our future, we do have much to fear? Attempting to have a child seems risky, no matter which course we select.

But God commands us to be "strong and courageous!" While we shouldn't make rash, unwise decisions, we can remain confident and unafraid of the challenges ahead. Our Lord commands us to put aside fear and discouragement and believe that He is more powerful than the problems we face.

How can you live out your faith today? I made it a habit to stop dwelling on the scary possibilities and to keep my eyes on Jesus. Maybe you need to make a phone call, or break a habit. Maybe you need to fill out paperwork from the adoption agency, or ask your insurance company about fertility coverage. The more time you spend thinking about the problem, the more your fears will multiply. Let your faith in God's great power move you beyond your fears into action.

---

*Lord, some people rush into bad decisions because they*
*have no fear. Others miss critical opportunities because*
*they feel too frightened to act. We know the secret lies*
*not in having courage alone, but having courage because*
*we have You. No enemy or decision is too big for us*
*because You are bigger still. Help us move today from*
*fear to freedom.*

# A COMPLETE FAMILY

*God saw all that He had made, and it was very good.*

GENESIS 1:31

How would you describe your life today, this life without children but with a spouse you love and who loves you?

"Okay."

"Pretty good."

"Not enough."

Do you want to know what God calls it? "VERY good." When the longing for a child becomes so intense that we grow unhappy with our marriage, we might wonder what God knows that we don't! Sometimes, unhappiness with our childless situation leaks over into unhappiness with our marriage and our spouse. It's far too easy to let our minds wander to a simpler time, before marriage, or to another sweetheart with whom we might have shared this life. We begin to confuse an external enemy — infertility — with an internal enemy, our spouse.

God created Adam and Eve to complete each other. God declared their marriage to be "very good" although they had conceived no children. God calls us, too, "very good" when we live in the holy union of a husband and wife. Authors Gary and Anne Ezzo remind us that we start a family when we say our wedding vows, not when conception occurs or we adopt a child. Gary and Anne Marie Ezzo write that "children do not complete a family, they expand it."[3] In God's eyes, you are already a completed family.

It's so easy to put all our time, energy and resources into the pursuit of having a child, but the needs of our marriage and of our spouse should always take precedence. If fertility treatments put too much pressure on one spouse, or if one spouse feels uncomfortable with the current plan of action, then make an immediate adjustment. Do whatever it takes to honor your spouse while you try to conceive. Consider dedicating one night a week to each other exclusively: no television, no discussion of children and pregnancy, no paperwork from the office. And above all else, make time every day to pray with and for each other.

You can enjoy a fullness in your heart and home by honoring your marriage as a completed family, blessed by God, and declared "very good."

---

*Lord, it's easy to feel that our marriage remains incomplete without children. Show us today how to honor our marriage as a complete family. Let Your words "very good" penetrate our spirits, our marriage, and our home. Help us to hold our heads high, knowing we have Your words of approval on our home and our lives.*

# AN UNWELCOME COMPANION

*Jesus replied, "You do not realize now what I am doing,*
*but later you will understand."*

JOHN 13:7

I have a confession. I know practically nothing about infertility. I don't know why God allows it. I don't know why He seems to be so silent sometimes. I don't know why women who don't want children get pregnant, and those who desperately want children remain childless. I don't know why some women who do crack every day while living on the streets give birth to one addicted baby after another, while other women who love God and live holy lives never get to feel a life growing inside their womb.

Even after suffering with infertility myself, I remain hopelessly uninformed. God just doesn't seem ready to hand out all the answers.

Confusion can be a constant, unwelcome companion on our journey to have a child. Sometimes no matter how often or sincerely we pray, we just don't seem to understand our situation or God's plan. Our limited view of an eternal God simply does not allow us to digest the sum of His actions.

It is true that confusion may remain for now; but later, when we see God face-to-face, we will understand everything. Choosing to believe in God now, and in His goodness despite the confusion and silence, may be the most courageous decision you will ever make.

---

*Lord, protect me from the hurtful effects of confusion. I do not understand what You are doing right now, but help me to develop an unwavering faith in You and Your plan for my life. You have promised me answers, even if I have to wait until eternity to see them revealed. Remind me that You do not act haphazardly or without care. Show me the order in the world around me, and remind me that I am a part of Your masterful work of planning and timely provision.*

# OBEDIENCE TO GOD'S LEADING

*March around the city once with all the armed men. Do this for six days. Have seven priests carry trumpets of rams' horns in front of the ark. On the seventh day, march around the city seven times, with the priests blowing the trumpets. When you hear them sound a long blast on the trumpets, have all the people give a loud shout; then the wall of the city will collapse.*

JOSHUA 6:3-5

Before the battle of Jericho ever began, God promised victory to Joshua's army. The Lord required a strange thing first, however: the army was to march around the city's wall seven times over seven days. Then the Israelites were to sound a trumpet blast before they had their victory.

I wonder, what did Joshua and his men think about these odd instructions? Can you imagine an army of fierce warriors, fearless as a band of Green Berets, loaded down with swords and armor and gathering around the campfire the night before they launched their attack — and hearing *that* set of orders? The soldiers learn they are to march around in a circle, then yell really loud while someone plays a horn. It had to sound more like a poorly orchestrated junior high pep rally than a brilliant military strategy. Were they being told how to attack a city, or do the hokey pokey?

Why the unusual battle plans? Perhaps God didn't want His men to fight the war themselves. But if so, then why didn't He just obliterate their enemies with a thunderbolt? We have to keep in mind that this perplexing, and perhaps even embarrassing, set of instructions came from a Strategist so great that He could have squashed Napoleon and MacArthur without breaking a sweat.

Has God been asking you to do some strange things lately? Maybe you've prayed for a child and He's asked you to take a break from medical treatments. Or He's encouraged you to keep pursuing medical help, yet as the months roll by, you've collected empty pill bottles, used syringes, and boxes of pregnancy tests — but no baby. In your battle for a child, God may ask you to do things that just don't make sense. It can frustrate us that He could correct our situation in the blink of an eye, and yet He asks us to march down paths that seem to lead us farther away from our cherished goal.

The role of faith is to reconcile our limited understanding with these strange divine directives. We must believe that His heavenly ways always remain the best, even when they don't seem to make any earthly sense.

------

*Lord, sometimes we get frustrated because we just want You to end the battle and bless us with a child without any further delay. We don't understand how or where You're leading us. Increase our faith so that we may joyfully follow You down any path, no matter how remote or off course it may seem. Please help us to clearly under-*

stand what You want us to do, and please give us a child
as we follow through on Your directives.

# WHY DID SHE LAUGH?

*Then the LORD said to Abraham, "Why did Sarah laugh and say,*
*'Will I really have a child, now that I am old?'*
*Is anything too hard for the LORD?*
*I will return to you at the appointed time next year*
*and Sarah will have a son."*

GENESIS 18:13-14

Sarah had passed her ninetieth birthday without ever being able to conceive, when God announced that she would deliver a baby boy within a year. Sarah laughed out loud when she heard this far-fetched prophecy. We can assume that long before she had made her peace with infertility and it seemed ridiculous to hope that God would turn her life around now. When God had not acted in the usual time to give her a child, she had said goodbye to that dream, forever.

Infertility challenges us in many ways, including the irritating fact that we seem to get so little information from God about why He allows it or what He plans to do about it. So we begin to read between the lines and fill in the gaps. We think we understand what He is up to in our lives — until He acts. Only then do we realize that He's on a completely different page!

Sarah watched as her fertile years slowly dripped away; then she passed through menopause and into old age. Her life's story said that she would never have a child, and so she closed the book. But God hadn't finished writing. He had a plot twist in mind so far out in left field that it would startle Sarah into a fit of laughter.

Isn't that what you are praying for today? A surprise ending so wonderful that you just have to laugh out loud?

It's only human to try to read God's mind and make sense of the events in our lives. But humans seldom do well at interpreting the divine. We never meet a moment when we know exactly what God will do. But a moment may well be approaching in your own life when the only possible response is to throw your head back and laugh.

---

*Lord, thank you for revealing to us through your Word that nothing is too hard for You. Thank you for the miracles of conception we read about in the Bible. They give us great hope! Help us to patiently wait to see what miracles will unfold for us. And finally, Lord, thank you that Sarah laughed, because we can believe that a sweet, bewildered joy awaits us the moment You overcome unbelievable odds.*

# A TURNING POINT OF FAITH

*Now my heart is troubled, and what shall I say? "Father, save me from this hour?" No, it was for this very reason I came to this hour.*
*Father, glorify your name!*

JOHN 12:27

Jesus dreaded His crucifixion, but God's incredible plan could not unfold without it. Jesus willingly endured shame, pain, and separation from God so that His Father would be glorified and His plan accomplished.

Are you crying out to God to be saved from this hour of infertility? God wants to hear the cries of our hearts, and He does listen. But consider for a moment what God might accomplish in you and through you. This crisis might be the turning point of your faith to unlock lifelong rivers of blessings. God may be shaping you for a great mission or preparing you to have a huge impact on the world around you. Perhaps God is simply molding you into a compassionate, wise parent for the children He will send you.

You may dread the pain of another day of waiting, of another cycle, of another childless holiday season. But you do not know and cannot anticipate what God will be able to do through you because you have endured this crisis.

---

*Lord, when we think waiting is futile and hope has grown hopeless, remind us that this crisis might be the most critical junction in our walk with You. Remind us of the miracles You are capable of and what You can do through a willing servant. We do not want to endure the pain of waiting, but may Your will be done. Father, glorify your name!*

# THE DECISION TO ADOPT

*Then the LORD God made a woman from the rib he had taken out of the man, and he brought her to the man.*

GENESIS 2:22

The decision to adopt can come hard after years of failed attempts to conceive. A husband or wife may need time to grieve that they could not conceive together. They may feel some hesitation about a child that "isn't ours."

When God created Adam, He used the dust from the ground. When God created Eve, He used a rib from Adam's side. And yet both were fully God's children. God's love made no distinction between them although they came into His family in different ways.

God has the right to give us children through any number of ways, and all are equally His and equally gifts from Him. We do not "own" a child because he or she developed in our womb. Each child is a gift from God.

A couple may also hesitate to adopt because of the added risks, such as birth mothers who return to reclaim a child, or unknown health histories. We fear losing the child through circumstances we cannot control.

But does having a child who comes from your womb offer any protection against loss? No. Only God can protect us and our children from the unknown, and we must trust Him with our sons and daughters, regardless of how God brings them to us. May God grant you peace and wisdom should you pursue adoption!

———————

*Lord, it may be time in our journey to consider adoption.*
*We confess we have many emotions to work through and*
*many fears and anxieties new to us. Thankfully, they are*
*not new to You. When fear clouds our thinking, calm us.*
*When pain fills our hearts, comfort us. Remind us that*
*all children come from You, as gifts. Please guide our*
*steps along this new path!*

# WHOSE FAULT IS IT?

*God has combined the members of the body and has given greater honor to the*
*parts that lacked it, so that there should be no division in the body, but that its*
*parts should have equal concern for each other.*
*If one part suffers, every part suffers with it;*
*if one part is honored, every part rejoices with it.*

1 CORINTHIANS 12:24-26

During a season of prolonged infertility, most couples seek out a
medical diagnosis to determine if they face any physical barriers to
conception. Their mindset becomes discovering "who has the
problem." If the wife's fallopian tubes are blocked, it's *her* problem.
If the man has a low sperm count, it's *his* problem.

The problem with this type of thinking is that it can erode the
unity of a marriage and foster feelings of resentment and guilt.
When you create a "his or hers" mentality in regard to infertility, you
can create small rifts in the intimacy and unity of your marriage.

We dare not forget that God proclaims a married couple to be
one flesh, one family unit comprised of two people (see Matthew
19:5). Therefore we must remain constantly vigilant to preserve a
"one flesh" attitude with our spouse.

Protecting your mate from feelings of guilt and inadequacy and avoiding the temptation to let others view the problem as "his" or "hers" honors your marriage and honors God. It allows God to continue to build your marriage into a safe haven for both of you. This can only better prepare you for His blessings ahead.

———————

*Lord, the world around us seems always to see infertility as either a woman's problem or a man's. Yet You see this as a problem both partners face equally. Please help us to see through Your eyes. Remove any trace of guilt, feelings of inadequacy, or anger. Help us to support each other and affirm our union.*

# PARENTHOOD IS NOT POSSESSION

*Then the Pharaoh gave this order to all his people: "Every boy that is born you*
*must throw into the Nile. . . ." When [Moses' mother]*
*could hide him no longer, she got a papyrus basket for him*
*and coated it with tar and pitch. Then she placed the child in it*
*and put it among the reeds along the bank of the Nile.*

EXODUS 1:22; 2:3

Even though Moses' mother defied Pharaoh's orders to kill her son, eventually she had to give him up to save his life. We can only vaguely imagine the heartache she must have felt as she said good-bye to her boy.

All of us must hold on to our dream for children with an open hand and a willing heart. Just as we do not know what God may require of us as we wait, we cannot know what he will require of us if we become parents. God does not promise us an easy, trouble-free path once we become pregnant or adopt.

Moses' mother reminds us that parenthood is not possession. We must struggle now to learn how to trust God with our lives, because we will have to trust Him later with our children's lives. Like so many of the great warriors of the Bible, you have been called to live with faith and without answers. It's not an easy life.

Not everyone is called to it. But when we bend with God's plan, God breaks our enemies. The surest way to defeat infertility is to trust God with it.

To save her son's life, Moses' mother had to let him go. She trusted God with her son and with her grief. She willingly endured the pain that comes from living without answers — and God responded by raising up Moses to lead all her people out of four hundred years of slavery. Praise the Lord for women who allow God to move in their lives even when it hurts!

————————

*Lord, cultivate in us an open, willing spirit. We do not know what lies ahead or what may happen if we do become parents. Thank you that Moses' mother had enough faith to risk her own life by disobeying Pharaoh, and faith enough to break her own heart in order to save her son. Grow our faith so that we can hold on to the dearest of blessings with trusting, open arms.*

# LETTING GO OF EXPECTATIONS

*And we know that in all things God works for the good of those who love him,*
*who have been called according to his purpose.*

ROMANS 8:28

What a blessed irony that God uses infertility to prepare us to be wonderful parents!

Infertility is often described as the death of a dream. When we first decide to become parents, most of us have a vision of our future family. We know how we'll discipline and guide our children; we imagine the good times and precious memories. But when children don't arrive according to our schedule and our plan begins to unravel, we must remember that God may be allowing our dreams to disappear from view only so He can show us what *He* has in mind. We must become willing to give our future children the freedom to pursue God's will for their lives, unfettered by our own selfish agendas.

As we wait for children, we come to understand, better than most, that children are gifts, not possessions. We learn to let go of our own expectations and let God's desires take center stage. As we wait for God's answer, we can develop a pliable, listening spirit to someday better hear the heart's cries of our children.

Someone once said, "God's answers are wiser than our prayers." How true! This season of waiting may seem unproductive, but God can use frustrating delays to create resources of wisdom and faith for you to draw upon later. Your future children need you to wait right now and to learn all the difficult lessons that infertility is teaching you, because these are the only lasting treasures you will pass on to them.

---

*Lord, when we complain about the hardships we experience, remind us that You are giving us great blessings as well. Butter, eggs, flour and plain sugar taste terrible to eat one by one, but when mixed under a skillful eye, they get transformed into something wonderful. In the same way, we may not like the individual ingredients You have given us, but we live under Your watchful eye and trust You for a wonderful result.*

# GOD IS IN CONTROL

*It does not, therefore, depend on man's desire or effort, but on God's mercy.*
ROMANS 9:16

While Romans 9:16 refers to our salvation through Christ, it also reminds us of Who must ultimately fight our battle of infertility. We can go to the doctors, take the drugs, do the procedures, pray and wish and want — but ultimately, God must do the work.

Many infertile couples receive chastisements from well-meaning observers to relax, start or stop exercising, or go on vacation — as if these things always produce a child. But only God can grant a pregnancy and our emotions and innocent activities do not limit His purpose and plan. The Lord can grant us a child whether we feel stressed out, overworked with no vacation, actively pursuing treatment or even taking time off from trying. Romans 9:16 reminds us that our desires and efforts are no match for God's mercy.

This takes much of the burden off our shoulders. Conception remains a miracle we cannot control or produce. The greatest reproductive scientists and the most skilled psychologists are just as much at the mercy of God's mystery as we are. And no one who claims to know the secret really understands the subject.

Lord, thank you that the burden of granting us a child remains in Your hands and off our shoulders. We will stay obedient to Your will and leading, but remind us that this battle is Yours alone. We will honor You in our efforts, confess to You our desires, and trust in Your mercy.

# God Is Aware

*I have indeed seen the misery of my people . . .*
*I am concerned about their suffering.*

Exodus 3:7

Do you ever feel as though God has forgotten you as you wait for a child? Does anger and resentment ever burn in your heart because it seems as though God is granting pregnancies to everyone else but you?

We do not know the reason God has not yet acted to grant you a pregnancy. Perhaps He is simply and silently waiting for the right time to reveal His gift. We do know that God has seen your misery as you wait month after month, and He is concerned about your suffering. Your suffering troubles Him because He loves you very much. We don't know why He hasn't yet removed the cause of the suffering, but you can have faith that He has not abandoned or forgotten you.

Your faith is being stretched today. Do you believe in God when He remains silent, when there seems little evidence that He actively intervenes or even exists? The answer is being revealed through your actions and emotions right at this moment.

*Lord, thank you for telling us that You see our suffering
and that it concerns You. We need to know that we
matter to You, that our wounds hurt You, too. Grant us
faith to believe in Your love despite
the lonely stretches of silence.*

# ANGELS AND OBSTACLES

*"Don't be afraid," the prophet answered. "Those who are with us are more than those who are with them." And Elisha prayed, "O LORD, open his eyes so he may see." Then the LORD opened the servant's eyes, and he looked and saw the hills full of horses and chariots of fire all around Elisha.*

2 KINGS 6:16-17

One afternoon my circumstances seemed overwhelming and unbearable. I started dwelling on what surely had to be my future: a bleak life filled with more frustration and hardships.

Not knowing what else to do to get my mind off my heartache, I opened the Bible, praying that God would somehow inspire me. I began reading the story of Elisha and his servant as they faced a hostile enemy army (see 2 Kings 6). Elisha and the servant appeared quite alone — until God opened the servant's eyes to see battalions of angels surrounding them.

*But what does this have to do with me?* I wondered. I didn't face an army. I faced uncertainty and a future that looked just as bleak as the unendurable present. I almost closed the Bible and walked away, but I pleaded with God to give me the encouragement I needed to get through the day. As I kept reading, God's words finally penetrated the thick haze of discouragement that had muddled my brain.

Yes, I had a different enemy than the one Elisha faced. But

God's angels *always* surround us and outnumber our enemies. That day I faced the enemy of discouragement and fear, but God's Word promised me that His grace and encouragement would outnumber and overthrow my doubts and fears.

To be honest, I did believe that — but I felt anxious to see it in action.

Later that afternoon, in what can only be a divine "coincidence," a neighbor dropped by unexpectedly. Although she and I were friends, our busy routines made lengthy conversations rare. She certainly didn't know what I had read that morning or how I was waiting to see God in action. But she had a surprise for me — she presented me with a beautiful, knitted white throw featuring an army of angels standing at attention!

Yes, God was indeed at work in my life. Already He had arranged His troops on the battlefield. He just needed to gently open my eyes.

---

*Lord, open my eyes today. I want, I need to see Your protection and provision all around me. The harsh enemies I face — doubt, fear, discouragement, negative test result — make me tremble. Sometimes I feel surrounded and doomed to defeat. Remind me to lift up my eyes to see how You are defending me every day.*

# FAITH IN AN UNSEEN GOD

*"I am the Lord's servant,"* Mary answered. *"May it be to me as you have said."*

LUKE 1:38

One day an angel appeared unexpectedly to a young peasant girl named Mary. The angel announced that she would become pregnant through a miracle of God prior to her pending marriage. He also instructed her to name her son Jesus.

In those days, an unmarried woman who became pregnant could be executed for immorality. Mary risked her life by agreeing to become the mother of Jesus — and she didn't even get to name the baby! The angel didn't offer to explain this divine arrangement to her fiancé or give Mary any reassurance that the marriage would still happen. In a few brief seconds Mary's plans for her life radically, irrevocably changed, and the angel didn't offer a single glimpse of how it would all turn out.

I would have asked to read the fine print; Mary responded with simple, immediate trust.

God may unveil a plan for your life without revealing any details about the ending. Perhaps His plan for you includes waiting, facing disappointments or malicious gossip. You naturally want to know how everything will work out in the end; God wants you simply to know Him in the present and trust Him with the unspoken ending.

It seems incredible to most of us to leave so much up to an unseen God, but that is what faith entails. If a young, uneducated girl can trust God even if it means facing ridicule, a broken engagement, and even death by stoning, surely we can find the courage to trust God with our desire to have a baby. We have everything and hope only to gain more; Mary had everything to lose and yet eagerly stood ready to give it all up at the sound of her Lord.

Now, that's faith — and that's what God irrevocably calls us toward.

---

*Lord, grant us faith! Mary had such amazing trust and faith in You to accept such an unexpected turn of events. In the same way, we didn't anticipate this path You are leading us down. Grant us enough faith to respond as Mary did: We are Your servants! May it be to us as You have said! Give us the kind of faith that allows You to accomplish whatever You desire in our lives. Use our faith to prepare us for a miracle. We trust You for the details of our lives, and for the ending as well.*

# IF ONLY

*I have learned the secret of being content in any and in every situation, whether well fed or hungry, whether living in plenty or in want.*
*I can do everything through him who gives me strength.*

PHILIPPIANS 4:12-13

Are you plagued with the "if onlys"? Do you often think, if only I could have a baby, I would be happy? If only God would grant this one request, everything would be fine?

I have. But you and I both know that things don't always work out the way we envision.

While waiting for the birth of her child, a dear friend of mine learned she suffered from an advanced stage of cancer. Pregnancy had created the perfect conditions for rapidly dividing cancer cells to flourish.

Another friend married a woman he deeply loved. They looked so happy together and soon after the wedding I attended a party she hosted at their new home. Every piece of furniture had been beautifully selected and she had laid out an attractive buffet for her guests. But she deserted her husband a few weeks later.

A couple I know finally bought the house of their dreams.

They left no detail overlooked and spared no expense. Then both lost their jobs.

"If only" is a one-sided affair. We refuse to admit the possibility of anything less than permanent euphoria once we attain our goal. We refuse to acknowledge that our present unhappiness could easily follow us into our future dream.

If you struggle to learn contentment now, you'll still struggle when you have children. If you struggle with anxiety and fear now, they won't magically disappear when you bring home a baby.

It's dangerous to stake our happiness on our circumstances. We simply don't know what lies ahead. Learning contentment in the here and now equips us to deal more effectively with what comes after.

---

*Lord, when I can't see the future, I naturally want to assume that it's got to be better than this! I don't want to postpone happiness — but don't let me postpone growing in You, either. Teach me the secret of being content, whether I have children yet or not. Give me the ability to thrive and enjoy every season of my life, so that if You grant me children in the days ahead, I'll be better prepared to savor the miracle You've given.*

# A FAITH THAT CRIPPLES

*All these people were still living by faith when they died.*
*They did not receive the things promised;*
*they only saw them and welcomed them from a distance.*
*And they admitted that they were aliens and strangers on earth.*

HEBREWS 11:13

A friend of mine who finally became pregnant after a long battle with infertility began to notice signs of a miscarriage. While she waited for a report from her doctor, she received an email that told her that if she "really believed" the Bible, it wasn't too late to pray and stop the miscarriage. The note insisted that if she just had enough faith, she could stop anything, change everything, and heal anyone through the sheer force of her will by prayer. The note deeply troubled my friend and caused her to fear that she might lose the baby if she didn't try hard enough to believe.

But I wonder: If we truly have received an independent power to change our lives as we see fit, doesn't this mean we have become divine ourselves? What need would we have for the real God? Doesn't that kind of "faith" cripple us instead of setting us free? We become responsible for all the bad that happens to us and feel we can take credit for all the good that comes our way.

Author and pastor Andy Stanley cuts quickly to the faultline of this type of faith: go to any children's hospital, look at the suffering, and ask yourself if you believe these children suffer because they lack faith.

Faith commands, it does not demand. Faith commands anxiety and doubt to flee. Faith commands our hearts to surrender our deepest desires, and believes we will receive God's richest blessing in return.

When you face trials and heartache, don't feel afraid to ask for what you want and how you want it. Expect God to answer your prayers. But expect God to orchestrate His answer according to *His* plan for your life. When we give God the greatest latitude in answering our prayers, we also give Him the greatest latitude to perform astonishing miracles and blessings.

---

*Lord, we face situations we don't understand and don't like. We wish we could escape by just saying "the magic words" or a certain prayer. We don't know why You have brought us to this hour. We want a child, but we don't want to interfere with Your precious, perfect timing or the miracle You are surely working in our lives as we wait. Please show us today what faith really is. Give us the courage to pray for something even greater than our own will: the desire to see You glorified through our waiting.*

# THE NECESSITY OF PERSISTENCE

*And will not God bring about justice for his chosen ones,*
*who cry out to him day and night? Will he keep putting them off?*
*I tell you, he will see that they get justice, and quickly.*

LUKE 18:7-8

My mother was an easy target. With a house full of kids and pets, she didn't have the fortitude to withstand the persistence of a determined child. In fact, that's how I got my first dog, my Barbie DreamHouse, and became a newspaper reporter at age twelve. If you just keep talking, I learned, sooner or later, somebody will listen.

Secretly, though, I wondered if I should call my persistence a flaw or an attribute. It seemed to me that adults called it by different names at different times. To a businessman, it was determination. To my mother, it was nagging — or as she called it, "wearing the bark off a tree."

How appropriate that, decades later, I would face the same question again. Was I nagging God to death and so spoiling any chance I had of getting a baby? Or did He admire my determination?

I began to get some answers through a parable Jesus told His disciples. In the tale of "the persistent widow," an indifferent, arrogant judge refused to handle a widow's case. The widow kept coming to his home and begging him to rule on her behalf. The judge finally agreed to grant her request, but only because he grew tired of her constant pestering. To an obstinate person like myself, that's what I'd call a win-win situation.

How do you picture God? Do you see God as the indifferent judge who must be worn down by your repeated prayers? Do you feel exhausted and even angry that your many pleas have gone unanswered and wonder if you should keep on asking? Jesus reassures us in this parable that if an evil judge can be swayed by sheer persistence, a loving God surely listens to repeated cries and, at the appropriate time, will move quickly to act.

The judge in this parable had no intention to help the widow, but acted only out of irritation at her persistence. God, on the other hand, has every intention of helping you. Jesus tells us not to lose heart as we "cry out to him day and night" because He *is* going to act on our behalf.

Your persistence will not wear God out or make Him angry. Don't be afraid to keep repeating your prayers and requests. It is His good pleasure to act on your behalf, in His perfect timing.

---

*Lord, You are so different from us! Thank You for reassuring us that we can't annoy or bother You with our constant pleas for Your intervention. Thank You that You have promised to act on our behalf. As we repeat our requests each day, reveal something new to us in return. Help us to see You at work all around us as we wait. Give us faith to continue to believe that You will act on our behalf as we wait for children.*

# TEMPTATIONS

*No temptation has seized you except what is common to man.*
*And God is faithful; he will not let you be tempted*
*beyond what you can bear. But when you are tempted,*
*he will also provide a way out so that you can stand up under it.*

1 CORINTHIANS 10:13

There's an old saying: "Trouble comes in threes." I don't think it's true, but I do know that one crisis can often precipitate another.

Infertility can cause many others problems to surface: jealousy, financial concerns, or impatience, just to name a few. Infertility can also cause certain temptations to seem irresistible — enticements that, under normal circumstances, you could avoid without much trouble.

I once participated in a Christian woman's infertility support group. Most of the women offered delightful inspiration, but a member of the group's leadership team surprised me when she began openly posting her requests to buy fertility drugs second-hand from other group members. This, despite the clearly typed federal warning on every package that only a pharmacist could legally sell these drugs.

You might never struggle with lying, but if an employer asks about time off, you may be tempted to make up a story. The stress that infertility places on your marriage can lower your resistance to other temptations as well. I work in an office full of men, and it's such a relief sometimes simply to enjoy their company and their goofy jokes, without struggling through difficult conversations or arguing about whether to take a month off from trying. I have to keep my mind on a short leash, or the next thing I know, it'll be walking *me!*

It may seem unfair that you have to walk through a minefield of ethical issues and temptations while struggling with the heartache of infertility. Infertility will force you to examine a thousand issues that you might never have considered otherwise. You and your spouse will have to see black and white in the shades of gray that surround you.

Once you have decided what is right and what is wrong in your particular situation, you may feel pushed to do the wrong thing by your exhausted emotions and by the high stakes of trying for a baby. But God has promised to provide a way of escape for every temptation and He has promised to meet our every need. We can obtain nothing by dishonest means that He cannot provide for us. A guilty conscience will only weigh down your already burdened heart.

---

*Lord, sometimes doing the wrong thing looks to be the
most expedient route to what we want. Help us to hold
on to our integrity no matter what it seems we lack. In*

*every situation, please provide for us something more*
*than we thought to ask for, both as a testimony to others*
*and to the inner voice that urges us to do wrong.*

# OFFERING OUR SCARS

*Then he said to Thomas, "Put your finger here; see my hands.*
*Reach out your hand and put it in my side. Stop doubting and believe."*

JOHN 20:27

Three days after Jesus died on the cross, He rose from the dead and appeared to His disciples. One disciple, Thomas, couldn't quite believe that Jesus had returned to life. So Jesus invited Thomas to touch the wounds from His crucifixion, and by examining His scars, to remove all doubt about His reality and message.

Do you suffer from the deep wounds of infertility, miscarriages, or other heartaches? Do you grieve because you bear the scars of these events? If so, the story of "doubting Thomas" offers you great hope. Thomas needed to see and touch Jesus' wounds before he could believe. But Jesus had to pass *His* test before Thomas could accept His words.

There are people in your life, too, who need to see your wounds before they will listen to you. But if they see your wounds — if you offer them your scars — they will begin to believe that you and your God are indeed real. Your scars can give you credibility among the wounded . . . if you allow others to see them.

Jesus also chose another surprisingly simple tactic to build the disciples' faith. He strengthened them simply by eating a meal with them. Sharing a meal proved Him to be real and not a ghost or a figment of their imagination.

Going about your normal routine of eating and working and living in the midst of suffering can help prove the reality of your faith, too, and that your God is present. So don't grieve because you have been wounded. Your wounds may be just what someone needs to see before *they* can believe. Don't assume that continuing your normal routine somehow diminishes the importance of your struggle. Instead, maintaining order amidst the chaos of pain draws people to you and your God.

God has amazing things planned for your life and unusual ways of expressing His presence to those around you. Your faith can take everyone by surprise when you give your sufferings to God.

---

*Lord, in our culture we shy away from showing our*
*wounds. We don't want people to know how deeply we*
*hurt. But someone out there may be hurting just as badly*
*and needs to see our scars. Give us wisdom to know when*
*to be vulnerable with others. When people see our faith*
*in spite of our scars, give them the courage to stop doubt-*
*ing that You exist! Thank you, Lord, that only You can*
*take devastation and turn it into deliverance. Give me*
*the courage, too, to keep putting one foot in front of the*

other. We pray that people would be moved by our ability to continue with a contented life and simple routine as we wait for Your blessing of a child.

We love you!

# WOBBLY FINANCES

*Yours, O LORD, is the greatness and the power and the glory and the majesty and the splendor, for everything in heaven and earth is yours. . . .*
*Wealth and honor come from you; you are the ruler of all things.*

1 CHRONICLES 29:11-12

Trying to overcome infertility can get expensive: medical tests, drugs, adoption fees, time away from work. Your financial resources may seem too small for such an expensive problem, and resentment can build towards those who have "more" or who have insurance with better fertility coverage. Financial pressure can strain an already burdened marriage, and when the pressure mounts, you may be tempted to act in less than honorable ways financially.

God is the God of finances. First Chronicles describes God as the possessor of greatness, power, majesty and splendor. He owns everything in heaven and earth. So is there anything too expensive for God? He owns it all.

Is your bank account too small for God to accomplish His plan for your life? He owns every bank account in the world. Is your employer unwilling to extend insurance benefits for fertility treatments? God rules over your company and over every other company, and no one's decisions or actions limit Him. No limits restrict what God can do, and if He plans to give you a child, no circumstance can thwart Him.

By the time my husband and I had reached the end of our financial rope, we still had no baby. There seemed no way to continue with medical treatments, and I felt exhausted spiritually from waiting on God to act on our behalf. As I walked to the mailbox one winter afternoon, the cold winds made the world feel as hostile toward me as I felt toward life. I knew I would have to face the end of my attempt to conceive because we simply couldn't afford to go on. Bitterness that comes from being so out of control over something so precious filled my heart.

I brought the mail in and read it by the fire, aimlessly tossing junk mail into the flames until I found an unexpected envelope from my grandmother. I adored her, although our conversations always had veered toward her recipe for rhubarb pie and our mutual love of tag sales. Never had we discussed finances.

Nonetheless, my grandmother's accountant had advised her that she could avoid a tax burden if she sent me a cash gift at the end of the year. The amount matched exactly what I needed to continue treatment. It also matched exactly what I needed to renew my spirits.

Who else but God could orchestrate a tax accountant's advice in another state, given months before, to impact me on the very day I most needed it?

---

*Lord, please help us to focus on who You are, not what we have. Whenever we feel pressure and fear, remind us of Your greatness, power, glory, majesty and splendor. When we face the "facts" of our financial situation, remind us of the truth: You own it all and You are working on our behalf, long before we even know we have a need. Thank You!*

# LOSING FAITH

*If we are faithless, he will remain faithful.*

2 TIMOTHY 2:13

Months and years of prayers that seem to go unanswered can wear down your faith. Although a lot of Christians don't seem to talk about it, it's not uncommon to go through a season of intense doubt and questioning.

You may question God's character or even if He really exists. Guilt and fear begin to control you because you don't think you can share these dark feelings and suspicions with anyone. Sometimes, your doubts grow so strong you fear you'll lose any chance of God granting you a child, for why shouldn't He punish you for your deep discouragement with Him and His timing? It just doesn't seem right to be a Christian and wrestle with such volatile emotions.

After my second child died in the womb, my rage against the world — and God — went unchecked. How could I continue praying to the God who chose to let this happen? How could I *ever* trust such a God?

I knew Him intellectually as good and loving, but did I really want to have anything to do with *this* kind of love, a love that could allow a car accident to take my first child and a miscarriage to take my second?

One night, surrounded by close friends, I let it all out. As I spoke, even my muscles flexed and tensed, as if ready to spring on an opponent. Where was my answer? Where was my God? The room remained silent for a bit, and then one dear friend asked if I wasn't really angry just because I hadn't gotten what I wanted.

I thought my head would spin around and fire would shoot from my nose. I wasn't asking God for a new car or a promotion at work; I was asking for a life to be spared! I was asking that God not let my heart get wrenched from my body as I said goodbye forever to my unborn child. It wasn't about me or what I wanted — it was about who God was and what was in His heart.

No one had a satisfactory answer for me that night; no one has since. Even Job, who endured the greatest heartbreak in the Bible, had to let his burning questions go by simply acknowledging that, "I talked about things I did not understand, about marvels too great for me to know" (Job 42:3, TEV). Like Job, I would receive no easy answers for my crisis of faith. Unlike Job, I had faithful friends who let me freely express my deepest doubts and confusion.

God reassures us that a crisis of faith does not change His love for us. James 1:17 promises that God "does not change like shifting shadows." He loves you when you're happy and He loves when you grow angry or discouraged. He listens to your prayers of gratitude and He listens to your complaints and tirades. Our faith — or lack of it — does not change His character or His intention toward us. Your emotions may determine the quality of the experience, but they won't determine the ending.

---

*Lord, it scares me to feel so far away from You. You are my only hope of deliverance. Please reassure me of Your compassion and concern even when I seem to have lost my faith. When discouragement and doubt overshadow the conviction of Your Presence, please wait patiently for me to find my way back to You. Help me to feel comfortable bringing everything to You — even my doubts about who You are and questions about why You have not yet granted me a child.*

# Who Controls Reproduction?

*This is what the LORD says to you:*
*"Do not be afraid or discouraged . . . for the battle is not yours, but God's."*
2 Chronicles 20:15

So few of our attempts to conceive a baby are in our control. We can take our temperature every morning and our medication every night, and still not be able to control our ovulation. We can count the days of our cycle, use the newest ovulation predictor technology and make love at just the right time, and still not get pregnant. Scientists can inject sperm into an egg in a laboratory, and even grow an embryo, but they still can't guarantee you a baby.

Only God completely controls reproduction.

Does it bother you to be completely at the mercy of an invisible God? We've all been programmed to take charge, make things happen, and get what we want. Acknowledging our dependency on God may frighten us, especially if our relationship with Him needs some work. How does God feel about us and about giving us a child? Can He be trusted to handle this crisis?

God knows that you face a battle with many enemies: emotions, finances, time, health. God does not want to fight *alongside* you; God wants to fight *for* you. God wants you to come off the battlefield and lay down your weary body and broken armor. He intends to march into battle and conquer your enemies while you watch. You have no promise that the outcome will turn out exactly as you envision, but we do know that God will win. God asks us to have courage and endurance while we wait for Him to triumph.

If you're growing weary from fighting infertility, perhaps it is because you were never meant to fight at all. How ironic that God promises we will win the battle . . . by getting off the battlefield. How perfect that an invisible God has total control over the unseen miracle of conception!

_____

*Lord, You say that when an enemy confronts me, it's Your battle to fight, not mine. Give me faith to trust in You and Your ability to conquer my enemies. When I feel tempted to try to control or force the situation to a conclusion, help me to remember to get off the battlefield and out of Your way. I cannot see the womb, and yet I know it is there. I cannot see You, either, but I know You are here. I will trust You today with what is unseen in my life.*

# SATISFIED!

*Satisfy us in the morning with your unfailing love,*
*that we may sing for joy and be glad all of our days.*

PSALM 90:14

Some days it takes more energy than others to get out of bed.

The agonizing, repetitive nature of infertility — doctor visits and blood tests, the same repeated prayers and the same strained hopes, waiting for the end of a cycle and waiting for the beginning of a cycle — means that on some mornings there just aren't enough answers to go around. On those days, depression can settle around us like the morning dew.

On a dreary morning like that, God says His unfailing love will "satisfy" us. What does it mean to be satisfied, to have just enough but no more? I think it means that it will be just enough to know that He loves me beyond my wildest imagination and that His love can never end. This knowledge promises to penetrate the fog of discouragement on any given morning. And although I usually don't even talk until lunch and my third cup of coffee, God promises to give me enough joy to sing and be glad.

Are you ready to sing today? Does God first need to satisfy you with his unfailing love? Then ask Him! God loves when we ask for

His wisdom and promises that He "gives generously to all without finding fault" (James 1:5). Ask God to reveal the evidence of His unfailing love in your life. Ask Him to show you what it means to be satisfied by His love.

----

*Lord, satisfy me today with Your love! I need a break from the relentless repetitions of infertility. Help me to set aside all my questions and dwell on the ultimate answer: Your unfailing love for me. These mornings when I feel satisfied with You bring such a welcome reprieve from the battle of infertility — please send more my way. Help me to pass these days of waiting with a song in my heart and gladness on my mind.*

# BE SURE OF YOUR HOPE

*Now faith is being sure of what we hope for and certain of what we do not see.*

HEBREWS 11:1

God can seem distant and impersonal when we see others having babies while we continue to wait. He doesn't seem to care or to be actively moving on our behalf.

But the truth is, He already has acted. He has ordained and written out every detail of every day that we face.

You want to have a child — any child! (But God has a specific child set apart for you.)

You want a child born at any time, any day, any hour, and the sooner the better! (But God has a specific day and hour already chosen.)

If God is bringing a child to you, He already knows that child completely. He knows if your child prefers dogs or cats and what he or she will eat for dinner on a Tuesday night ten years from now. He knows when this baby will be conceived, what you'll be thinking when you hold your child for the first time, and how you're going to decorate the nursery. We wait blindly, but with faith; God sees everything and promises to remain faithful.

Faith is "being sure of what we hope for." Are you sure of your hope? Do you believe that God is fully capable of answering your prayers? And are you sure of what you're hoping for?

Infertility can cause a simple problem — the so-far unfulfilled desire for a child — to become a tangled knot of pleas. For what are you hoping today? Is it more than a child? There may be no physical evidence to prove that God is working to bring you a baby. Perhaps you are hoping for reassurance of God's power and control. So ask Him. Maybe you need some rest from the battle and a good laugh. So ask Him!

---

*Lord, we dream of having any baby and You tell us You are planning a specific child. We see senseless waiting; You see a Master Plan. Give us the faith to ask not for our will, but for Yours. Only You know why we wait, and only You know who we're waiting for. Thank you for being a God of specifics. Give us the faith to continue to wait, knowing no detail has escaped Your attention.*

# BABY SHOWERS

*Rejoice with those who rejoice; mourn with those who mourn.*

ROMANS 12:15

Is it wrong to stay home from a baby shower of a close friend? Are we being selfish if we refuse to attend these celebrations of pregnancy and impending birth? The answer depends on what's in your heart.

God judges us by our motives as well as our actions. If you want to stay home because you know you will cry and make the guests uncomfortable, you make a beautiful sacrifice to stay home. If you don't want to go because you secretly begrudge the woman her pregnancy, and if you feel angry that someone else got blessed first, then you are refusing to attend out of spite. What lives in our hearts when we take action is just as important as what we actually do.

I've sat through baby showers with my heart breaking, and I've made the mistake of attending a baby dedication before I was emotionally ready. I felt so glad I attended the showers because I demonstrated a commitment to my friends; it cemented our friendship when I could celebrate for them what I had not been given. I felt sorry I attended the dedication, because I had to leave when the tears came, and the host did not say anything to me later. The incident made our friendship awkward and diminished the pleasure of asking her to help me celebrate the milestones in my own life.

God encourages us to keep pace with our friends by celebrating their victories and mourning their losses, just as we would want them to keep pace with us. We want our friends to show us compassion when we suffer, and we will want them there when we celebrate the birth of our baby. If we begrudge them their happiness now, will they be there for our happiness later?

If you can keep pace — at least externally — with the emotions of those around you, then go and celebrate. God will see your sacrifice and bless you for your compassion. If you can't, God will not judge you harshly for not going, and so neither should you judge yourself. Set aside the time that would be spent at the shower to pour out your heart to God. Rant, cry, or write in a journal and open your wounds to the only One who can comfort you in the deepest longings of your heart.

---

*Lord, I want to do the right thing, not just for me, but for the guest of honor. Will my heartbreak overshadow her joy? Only You can help me decide that. Thank you for not judging me based on the external decision I make. Thank you that You have a plan to bless me and see me through whatever decision is appropriate. And please continue to move me toward the day when I, too, will celebrate the birth of my own child.*

# COMPARING PAINS

*Isaac trembled violently and said, "Who was it [that] I blessed . . . and indeed he will be blessed!" When Esau heard his father's words, he burst out with a loud and bitter cry and said to his father,*
*"Bless me — me too, my father!"*

GENESIS 27:33-34

Do you ever compare your pain to that of someone else? If you've waited for a child for three years and they've waited only one, then surely your pain is greater and more important, isn't it? If they have one child and you have none, then your pain should take precedence, shouldn't it?

It can be a wonderful comfort to speak with others who have suffered similar heartache, but when the conversation turns to comparing and quantifying each person's suffering, everyone walks away from the conversation diminished. The truth is, just as we can never fully know another person's heart and inner life, we can never fully understand their suffering.

When someone asks about how long we've waited and what we've experienced, and we suspect it is solely for the purpose of comparison, we need to acknowledge their pain in a graceful, compassionate manner. God does not operate on a "first come, first served" basis and His plan for your family does not change because of what others receive. The blessings He grants someone else do not lessen what He has in store for you, just as the length of someone else's suffering does not take precedence over your prayers when He answers requests.

Sometimes our desire to judge another's pain derives from an intense need to believe we can somehow capture God's attention — and His blessings — by suffering the most. We want His blessing at any cost and don't want anyone else to butt in line before us. Whatever it takes, we want to be the next person to receive a child from God.

Our story seems very much like that of Jacob and Esau. In those days, a father gave all of his possessions and privileges to his oldest son in the form of a "blessing." Jacob, the younger son, determined to gain these blessings. So Jacob dressed in his brother's clothes and even created false hair on his arms to mimic his brother's hairy skin, then went to his blind father to ask for the blessing. Isaac did not recognize the deceit and so blessed the wrong son. Jacob "butted in line" for the blessing before Esau, resulting in chaos and heartache for everyone, including himself.

Others do not have what you want. If you hope to win a prize by suffering the most or enduring the longest, you're going to be disappointed. The only One who can truly acknowledge your difficult journey is God alone. The only One with the blessing for you is God, and you must wait on His timing.

Lord, help me to acknowledge the suffering of those around me in a way that makes them feel affirmed and cared for. Help me to remember that Your plan for my life and family operates independently of what anyone else may experience. I am not competing for blessings. Encourage me to reach out to comfort those who mourn, even if their pain seems "less than" my own. Help me to celebrate another's blessings even while I still must wait for my own.

# LOOKING FOR SIGNS

*Then some of the Pharisees and teachers of the law said to him,*
*"Teacher, we want to see a miraculous sign from you."*
*[Jesus] answered, "A wicked and adulterous generation asks for a sign!"*

MATTHEW 12:38-39

We can get so desperate for a hint of what our future holds that we erroneously begin to read supernatural meaning into mundane moments. A certain song plays at a particular moment, our Bible falls open to a certain verse, or a card arrives from a friend who "just knows" this is the month for us to conceive.

Sometimes God does give us supernatural glimpses into what He is about to do in our lives, but if we crave these foreshadowings, we will begin to see them everywhere. These "signs" will cause us to become what Jesus described as "adulterous": turning aside from God to anything or anyone who promises to reveal our future. Faith will become frivolous and based on coincidence, not connection with God.

Author Jill Baughan, in her book, *A Hope Deferred: A Couple's Guide to Coping with Infertility,* recounts her disappointing experience with looking for signs:

> *I remember one December a couple of years ago, Ben and I were*
> *lying quietly in bed when he suddenly said, "This is it!" "What is?" I*
> *sat straight up, thinking he was about to get sick. "This month. This*
> *is the month you'll get pregnant. I know it, I feel it. I'm sure of it."*
> *Now you might expect this kind of statement from me — but Ben is*
> *an engineer. He thinks in straight lines. He's calm, rational, emotion-*
> *ally controlled. "Are you sure?" I asked, wanting badly to believe him.*
> *"Absolutely." And so began a month of positive "signs."*[4]

When Jill did not get pregnant after all, she recounts that her faith, and the faith of her husband, took a hard blow. She learned through this painful mistake that "our prayers do not go unanswered; we just misunderstood his answers."[5]

Seeking after signs instead of the Son will open you to misleading paths, disillusionment, and embarrassment. If you crave a sign today, you may need your faith strengthened that God is still listening, that He is still acting on your behalf. Look up verses in the Bible that comfort you and promise you His presence and divine care. You can stake all your hopes in God's promise of faithfulness in all circumstances, receive supernatural strength and comfort, and protect yourself from unnecessary heartache.

---

> *Lord, at times I would just give anything for a sign of*
> *what You are about to do. But when I feel this way, I*
> *know I am vulnerable to going astray and opening myself*

to disappointment. It must hurt Your feelings, too, that I look for supernatural insight in earthly coincidences. Please help me to focus on the real and true signs You've given me in Your Word. Help me to not fall prey to false signs, but to be thrilled as I see Your Word coming true not only in the circumstances of my life, but in the character of my heart.

# WAITING DOESN'T
# MEAN WORTHLESS

*But for Adam no suitable helper was found. . . . Then the LORD God made a*
*woman from the rib he had taken out of the man,*
*and he brought her to the man . . . and they will become one flesh.*

GENESIS 2:20-24

Sometimes, the wait for children can seem interminable, nudging a childless couple into dark feelings of worthlessness. Yet the Bible makes it clear that having children does not make a family better in the sight of God; it just makes it bigger.

Remember that God did not create Adam and Eve until the sixth day, after all the earth and the animals already had been made. So then, did the fact that Adam and Eve came after everything else — in fact, God waited to make them — imply they were less important than plants and animal life? Hardly! God first put everything else in its place specifically to prepare for their arrival. The timing of Adam and Eve's "birth" was the last *but most important act* in the events of the seven days of creation. God paved the way for their coming by designing and creating everything they needed for a happy and successful life in the garden.

In the same way, because God places great esteem on your

marriage, He is busily creating a place exactly suitable for you and your spouse. Never allow yourself to imagine that your waiting for children somehow impugns God's character or demeans your standing before Him. Instead, see it as part of His incredible orchestration of creation.

Your current waiting does not imply the least amount of personal worthlessness. Much to the contrary, it demonstrates the great lengths to which God will go to in order to create a place "just right" for your family to thrive. You can rest, reassured that you and your spouse are just as important to God as a couple with children. He promises to give you His full attention and provision, despite your troubled feelings.

---

*Lord, help us to know deep in our hearts that our waiting does not imply our worthlessness or that You place greater value on those with children. This longing we feel for children does not mean we are somehow less important than families with children. Help us to see the awesome privilege of waiting as You orchestrate all of creation to fulfill Your purpose for our lives.*

# WHAT KIND OF PROMISE IS *THIS*?

*He raises the poor from the dust*
*    and lifts the needy from the ash heap;*
*he seats them with princes . . .*
*He settles the barren woman in her home*
*    as a happy mother of children.*
*Praise the* LORD.

PSALM 113:7-9

Do you feel betrayed when you read a verse like the one above?
Does it seem as though God has promised to make all barren
women into mothers . . . but somehow has forgotten to include you
in His plan? If He delights in giving children to those who have
none, why isn't He giving you any? Where have you gone wrong?

It may seem to you as though God has taken out a full-page ad
to proclaim His ability to give you children — but then you read the
fine print and see that He has no intention of actually following
through on the promise in your case. Where's the truth in all of
this? Is there something amiss in your relationship, or in your inter-
pretation of this verse?

First, Psalm 113:9 *is* a promise from God. God promises that all
the ills that plague us — cultural, financial, and physical — remain

under His authority and will one day be removed. But God doesn't want us to read this verse and suppose that it gives us hope only for our future in eternity. God wants us to see that His power thunders forth not only in the heavens, but on earth as well. God wants to open our eyes to what is possible for Him at any moment. Too often we look around and confuse present reality with unchanging Truth.

Reality tells us that a homeless man isn't going to get an invitation to the Inaugural Ball. The Truth expressed in Psalm 113 is that God *could* put him there, and at the President's table, this very night. In your case, the reality is that, today, you wait for a child; the Truth is that God might put a child in your arms at any moment and in any way.

Reality can sometimes get in the way of Truth. Corporate trainers forever prompt their employees to "think outside the box." God wants you to do the same with Him! That's what faith is — not demanding what must happen, but assuming the impossible can become plausible through God.

While Psalm 113:9 states God's intention toward barren women, it does not necessarily declare His plan. Infertility is never God's idea of a good time; He does not like injustice and pain to clutter our lives. God knows how sweet it is to a barren woman to feel blessed with children. God will remove some of our burdens during our earthly lives, but He will not remove others until we join Him in eternity. God promises to make all things right in His time and in His way. Others may not understand the pain we feel, but God does, and He promises to make it right with us. If not now, then someday.

Praise the Lord that we have a God who understands the longing we feel for children and who delights in satisfying the desires of our hearts. God knows your deepest desires and your greatest needs. He has committed Himself to seeing the purpose of your life fulfilled — but you have to trust Him as the details unfold.

---

*Lord, what do You want us to learn from this Psalm?*
*We know You are capable and You imply that you are*
*willing — so why must we wait? You have convinced us*
*that You are a compassionate God who hates suffering,*
*so we ask again that You please settle us in homes happy*
*with children. We praise You for Your tender mercy and*
*ask You to grant us the desire of our hearts. When the*
*sting of the injustice of barrenness becomes too sharp,*
*remind us that You will not let injustice rule forever.*
*Help us to look beyond the reality facing us, to the Truth*
*of who You are and what You are capable of doing at*
*any moment.*

# GOD'S BOOK OF TEARS

*You know how troubled I am; you have kept a record of my tears.*
*Aren't they listed in your book?*

PSALM 56:8, TEV

Did you know that you move God? He rejoices at your smile and your tears tug at His heart. In fact, God has recorded every tear you have ever shed.

You probably can't recall every incident you've ever cried over. God not only remembers the event, but He knows exactly how many tears you cried! He knows from moment to moment what you're thinking and feeling, how many hairs populate your head, what you're craving for dinner, and when your favorite song is going to come on the radio. He is intimately wrapped up in the details of your life as He watches over you. When you feel tempted to believe He doesn't see you, consider instead that He may be so close that you can't see Him!

We need to begin to grasp this overwhelming love that surrounds us if we are to grow in our faith during a crisis. How could you trust a remote and indifferent god? What hope could you have as you prayed for such a god to hear you?

But our God is different. God is ever present and never weary. He put the heavens in place but still is moved by the single tear that rolls down your cheek. You can trust a God like that! Even if that means waiting for the child you long to hold. The delicate balance between knowing how much He loves you, and of His limitless power, can give you the courage to trust Him to care for and deliver you in His perfect timing.

———————————

*Lord, You are indeed the God of the impossible, for it seems impossible that the God who calls out the stars one by one has also made note of every tear I've shed. Although You are majesty beyond comprehension, Your heart goes out to me when I cry. I can trust You because no detail of our situation has escaped Your attention and You don't like to see us suffering for no purpose. Show me how tender and how powerful You truly are. I need to believe that You are able to overcome all our obstacles, and I need to believe You respond with compassion when I weep.*

# A SUPERNATURAL SALVE

*For the word of God is living and active. Sharper than any double-edged sword, it penetrates even to dividing soul and spirit, joints and marrow.*

HEBREWS 4:12

Struggling to have a child can be a lonely, isolating experience. Close friends cannot find the words that comfort us, and on some days even our spouses flounder for what we most need to hear. And even when someone speaks perfect words, when we feel loving arms wrapped around us at just the right moment, there remains an empty, sorrowful space they cannot reach.

I see this principle at work in my life. It frustrates my friends to offer their greatest condolences and richest words of wisdom, and yet know they cannot ultimately provide much help. My heart agonizes that although everyone has the answers, no one has a solution. No one can completely comfort and heal my broken heart.

That's why I need to hear God's promise that His Word is supernaturally alive and active. Only the supernatural can penetrate to this secret yearning space in my soul and grant me the reprieve from suffering that I crave.

When my body hurts from treatment, and yet my womb

remains empty; when my intimate relationships seem as impossibly distant as the child I long to hold — I need to know that the Bible verses I recite do not merely reside in my mind. They penetrate throughout my body, rooting out darkness and unleashing the light and power of a living God.

Words from human gurus and mystics are just words, but a word from the Lord acts as supernatural salve with the power to heal a ravaged heart. There is no mantra, no lotus position, no other "spiritual" writing that can equal this scriptural claim: to be alive and active, able to distinguish between emotion and spirit, joints and marrow, and to heal them all.

Never forget that when you open your Bible, you open your physical body, spirit, mind, and emotions to the transformation of a dynamic encounter with the Living God.

-----

*Lord, what would I do without You? Friends fail me,*
*loved ones fail me, religious pretense fails me,*
*and I fail myself in trying to get the comfort*
*I know I need. But Your Word lives and actively*
*works within me even as I read this. You are*
*strengthening me, comforting me, preparing me,*
*and soothing me. Nothing else compares to You.*
*Let Your Word penetrate my being today.*
*Divide and root out what does not belong.*
*Find the hidden longings and secret sorrows*
*and bring them into Your light. Make my healing*

*a marvelous example of what only Your Word*
*can do in a wounded soul.*

# HE LISTENS

*I love the LORD, because he hears me; he listens to my prayers.*
*He listens to me every time I call out to him. I kept on believing,*
*even when I said, "I am completely crushed."*

PSALM 116:1-2,10, TEV

Have you considered the important difference between hearing and listening? I *hear* background noise; I *listen* when people tell me they love me. When I was growing up, I *heard* my dad telling me to hang up the phone, while I *listened* to my girlfriends telling me who had crushes on each other.

We all know the difference between merely hearing and actively listening. God does, too, and He wants to assure you that He is listening. The Lord does hear you every time you pray. In fact, He doesn't just hear; he *listens*.

A person who really listens wants to hear your story in its entirety. A good listener doesn't rush or finish your sentences for you to hurry your tale along. Don't you just love a friend who will sit with you and let you pour out your heart, without interruption or distraction? That's how God listens to you as you pray; always willing to hear more, never in a hurry for you to finish. He may be

God, but He has the time to listen to our version of the events in our lives and how we feel.

It's so important that this truth about God listening to your prayers becomes a reality to you. Try to meditate on this verse today; memorize it or post it where you can see it. When you reach the point that you mimic the writer's cries — when you lament that "I am completely crushed" — you will need to keep on believing, just as the writer did. You need to keep on believing that God has listened and has not stopped up His ears. You need to believe He wants to hear more and wants you to draw close to Him, especially now.

To doubt whether God listens is to doubt whether He cares. Remind yourself that He is a friend who always feels sorry when the conversation has to end.

———————

*Lord, give me the strength to believe You are there, listening for my voice, even when I feel in the depths of despair. Give me the confidence to cry out! Change my image of You until it comes in line with the reality expressed in Your Word. You are a loving God who never tires of me. You actively listen when I call. What other "god" has such an incredible open-door policy? Grant me peace with the mystery that You are a God who always actively listens, but who nevertheless does not always reveal Himself. Help me to have the courage to*

*confide in You the deepest longings of my heart, knowing*
*that You may not fulfill them as quickly as I may desire.*
*Let me take comfort today in knowing that*
*I have been heard.*

# BE CAREFUL WHAT YOU ASK FOR

*So he gave them what they asked for,*
*but sent a wasting disease upon them.*

PSALM 106:15

One day, when the monotony of my life and the battles of infertility weighed me down, I prayed for a distraction. Things had gone unchanged for so long that I felt numb. I needed something to get my blood pumping again, to make me feel alive and energized.

Have you ever heard the expression "Be careful what you pray for"? That was true in my case.

That week I walked dinner down to a neighbor who had just given birth. After a nice visit I said goodbye, but as I turned to walk back home, a giant groundhog sprang from the bushes. He appeared to be about forty pounds and looked like a hostile, furred ottoman. Construction had recently disturbed his nearby nest and he seemed out for vengeance.

His wild, beady eyes swept up and down the block, as if to make certain I was alone. Then the beast scrambled toward me, surprisingly fast for a fat squat of a rodent. I screamed and tried to run, but his claws gave him an edge in the wet Georgia clay. Neighbors ran out from their houses, and, mercifully, an elderly woman ran out brandishing a broom to save me. It took about five people and ten minutes before the attacker decided that he had made enough sport of me, and he ran back into the trees behind my property.

We never saw him again, but I will never forget him, either.

God answered my prayer that week — my blood got pumping, my heart raced, and I learned my lesson about being a little more "certain" of what I prayed for!

What is it that you long for today? Can you narrow your longings down to a specific request? The more specific you get, the more clearly you'll recognize God's answer. And God loves to send specific answers to increase your faith and so that you'll know He attentively listens to every prayer. If you can't name anything specific, it's okay to leave the answer up to God — but just remember, a groundhog probably lives near you, too.

———————

*Lord, there are days when I feel so numb from the monotony of waiting that I need something to shake me awake. I'm not asking for a groundhog experience, but I need to know that You do indeed listen to my every prayer. Help me find one specific thing to pray for today, and let me clearly recognize Your answer. I want to feel truly alive and energized, not because my circumstances have changed, but because I know You are near.*

# BITTER COMPETITION

*Then Rachel said, "I have had a great struggle with my sister, and I have won."*
GENESIS 30:8

Rachel and her sister, Leah, both yearned for children. Leah succeeded but Rachel remained barren. While they didn't share a loving relationship, they did share one trait: the drive to compete against each other, no matter what damage it did to themselves or their families.

Their bitter sibling rivalry built to a white-hot degree when Leah alone conceived. Rachel reacted by taking drastic action. She instructed one of her maids to sleep with her husband, so the maid could have children in Rachel's place! Rachel refused to overcome her flaw of competitiveness; she focused too much on overcoming her sister. As a result, Rachel complicated her life and the lives of the entire family by encouraging polygamy. Rachel shortchanged herself out of her husband's time and affection. Ironically, the Lord's plan for Rachel did include pregnancy and children — just not at that moment.

Rachel's actions had far-reaching consequences. She eventually became the mother of Joseph, one of the greatest figures in Jewish history. Joseph saved many lives during a great famine and became the second most powerful man in the world. But Rachel's tendency to compete against others in her family directly affected Joseph and eventually caused him great pain. His half-brothers grew so intensely jealous of Joseph that their rivalry prompted them to sell him into slavery. They lied to Rachel that a wild animal had killed her son and Rachel never got to see her son grow up.

Competition with our "sisters," whether biological or just friends, can only complicate our lives and set in motion a chain of events that can break our hearts long after the rivalry is forgotten.

I know that if you have been unable to conceive, it hurts to see someone else pregnant. The wound feels almost unbearable if the other woman flaunts her pregnancy, takes it for granted, or treats our infertility as a trivial matter. We can retaliate out of desperation, a sense of powerlessness, and grief. I am guilty of competing against my sisters who conceived when I could not. I retaliated by flaunting my income and freedom and conspicuously indulging in expensive hobbies. My attempt to hide my pain created more heartache for everyone and drove others away. Competition complicates our lives. Years later, the relationships I destroyed were mended — but they remain damaged.

Why compete over something you can't control? If you do not master this urge to measure yourself against others, it will only intensify once children join your family. You will have no way of controlling the far-reaching consequences of competition.

When you feel tempted to retaliate and compete against a sister, remind yourself that you are establishing a home today for your children of tomorrow. If you want to lay a foundation of freedom for your children, you must not compete. Allow them to become who they were meant to be, without the pressure of measuring themselves against their peers.

---

*Lord, if I can't help but compete for my own sake, stop me from competing for my future children's. You give out of a limitless supply; what You give to another does not diminish what You have for me. Help me to forgive when I need to and turn away when I have to. Bless my relationships with my sisters here on this earth, and remind me to look to heaven for everything I want and need. If I have unknowingly set in motion harmful events because of my urge to compete and compare, please stop those events now. Heal me and heal the relationships in my life. When I feel sibling rivalry creeping up, grant me the strength of character to bless my sister for her blessings, instead of cursing her for having what I want.*

# FINISH THE RACE

*Therefore, since we are surrounded by such a great cloud of witnesses,*
*let us throw off everything that hinders and the sin that so easily entangles, and let*
*us run with perseverance the race marked out for us.*

HEBREWS 12:1

I once entered a 10k race, a running competition a bit over six miles long. I didn't train for it, other than buying some running shoes and a clever new jogging outfit shortly before the race.

Weather forecasters predicted an extremely hot weekend for the event, but that didn't trouble me. After all, the material in my running jacket featured a new synthetic blend guaranteed to wick moisture away from the skin. I had everything I needed to finish this race under my own power.

And don't think I had given little thought to the rigors of endurance the race would place upon my body! I also had purchased waterproof mascara and eight-hour lipcolor. And because I was single at the time, I carefully left my eyeglasses at home the morning of the race. I dwelled on appearances when I should have focused on mechanics.

But when the starting gun sounded, I took off. Never mind that by the end of the first half hour, I had to shed my stunning new running jacket. It had wicked moisture away from my skin, all right — by making me sweat until perspiration ran like rivers down my back. Women pushing baby strollers while chatting it up on their cell phones left me in the dust. Whole platoons of weight loss clubs passed me by.

The heat bore down on me and my energy reserves felt tapped out. As I rounded a street corner I saw a glorious neon race marker. *I'm half way there!* I rejoiced. Sure, it was much harder than I imagined, but I could finish, now that I had the end in sight. I was doing *great!*

As I neared the sign, however, my nearsighted eyes finally made out what it actually said: "I MILE." I had completed only a single mile — five more yet to go!

God describes your life today as a race, with you as a runner. He created the racecourse and you as the runner, and He wants you to fare better than I did in that hot, humid race so long ago. He knows everything about how you should prepare for your race and how you should run it. It may seem as if you have further to run than you have strength to draw upon, but that's where endurance and perseverance come in. You *can* finish the race — just so long as you continue to depend on the One who calls you to the finish line.

―――――――――

*Lord, daily living with infertility feels like running a marathon in slow motion. I get so exhausted, and everyone, it seems, fares better than me at having babies. Some days all I want to do is sit down and cry — but* even so, I have to keep moving. I have to know what's at the end of my finish line. Thank you, God, that You are not a coach who judges from the sidelines or yells encouragement from a distance. You are the Friend who runs beside me, and You are strong enough to carry me when my own strength gives out.

# TRAINING TIPS

*Do you not know that in a race all the runners run,*
*but only one gets the prize? Run in such a way as to get the prize.*

1 CORINTHIANS 9:24

I learned a number of hard lessons on that day so long ago when I set out to run a 10K race, armed only with a fashionable running jacket and waterproof mascara. And I'd like to offer for your consideration four training tips that God seared into my brain, applicable not only to road races but, more importantly, to the race of life.

First, you can't run a marathon wearing a parka. God calls you to peel off the layers of self-sufficiency, pride, doubt, and envy that weigh you down and keep you from peak performance. My running jacket looked great, but it almost cost me the opportunity to finish the race. I had to let it go if I intended to keep moving forward.

Second, you need to run with perseverance. You'll need endurance for this race — God doesn't gloss over how hard it is. But remember, if He tells you to run with perseverance, He'll make sure you have the strength to do it. I know the despair of running out of steam long before the race ends. God promises that when we allow Him to coach us, our endurance will perfectly match the contours of the course.

Third, God instructs you to focus on the path marked out for you. He has clearly marked out the course; you must follow the turns and dips set out for you. No matter what your emotions tell you, you do not have to wander aimlessly so long as you remain on course. When I ran my 10k, I could not afford to focus on outside distractions or on what people on the sidelines were yelling (although I think they wanted to know if I needed a medic). I just had to keep forcing my legs to move, to follow the path little by little (and pray that the end of the race would be mercifully near!).

And the most wonderful lesson of all: God has supplied a cheering section. All the residents of heaven who finished their races, and who know the difficulties you face, surround you as you plod along, cheering you to stay the course and win your race. Can you picture spectators crowding the sidelines? Sometimes, all you need to keep putting one foot in front of the other is the knowledge that someone is watching and cheering for you to press through the pain.

———

*Lord, I take comfort in knowing that You, and not my
enemies, have laid out the course of this race. You know
this path intimately and You know me completely.
Grant me perseverance! Help me to keep putting one
foot in front of the other. And when my strength seems*

*gone, help me imagine what my cheering section must look like. Give me a refreshing laugh and the spark to continue, knowing I am loved on earth and in heaven.*

# SMALL SACRIFICES

*But when you give to the needy, do not let your left hand know what your right hand is doing, so that your giving may be in secret.*
*Then your Father, who sees what is done in secret, will reward you.*
MATTHEW 6:3-4

I had lunch one afternoon with a girlfriend burdened down by the demands of rearing two active little boys. Her husband was traveling and she felt bone-tired and in need of some encouragement. We didn't discuss what mattered most to me, the burdens of my heart on my own journey. My silence — a rare event! — was a sacrifice I gave to God.

When I've sat through baby showers with a smile plastered on my face or endured phone conversations with friends who droned on about their kids, it was a sacrifice I gave to God. There is a time and place to reveal these emotions and struggles with our friends, but some days, people get so wrapped up in their own dramas that to add my own burden to the mix would poorly serve both of us. They wouldn't know what to say and I wouldn't feel supported.

I have to recognize when friends become too needy to help me. In this way, I secretly bless my friends. I give to the Lord the secret sacrifice of my pain, instead of burdening my friend with it. But

God sees what I do in secret and promises to reward me.

Some sacrifices get everyone's attention and respect — a soldier who lays down his life to preserve freedom, a husband who leaves his career to care for an ailing wife. It can be hard to imagine that the small, sometimes daily sacrifices that I make are worthy of similar honor and reward. But God always works in unexpected ways. We may value great sacrifices given publicly, but God places just as much honor on "small" gifts given in secret.

We can give back to God in many ways. We can offer God our finances, our time, and our abilities. But the small, secret sacrifices we make are often the hardest.

What small, secret sacrifice are you making? Did you offer a smile and a word of encouragement to an unwed teenage mother? Did you respond with patience and grace when a busybody demanded to know why you didn't have kids? Maybe you listened to another's troubles on a day when your heart felt heavy from the burdens of infertility. God wants you to know that He sees these small acts of courage and kindness. He knows you intimately and understands what a sacrifice you make when you care for those who miss your pain. God promises you both recognition and reward!

———————

*Lord, people often feel so free to discuss trivial matters and it can seem unfair that we must sometimes keep our burdens to ourselves. Help us not to begrudge our friends who lack either the time or ability to comfort us. And remind us that extending these little graces to our friends* will never go unseen or unrewarded. Thank you that nothing escapes Your watchful eye. Thank you for being so intimately acquainted with our ways that You understand how the "little things" can sometimes be the hardest. Thank you for giving us something better than justice or equity: Your mercy.

# LET DREAMERS DREAM

*Bear with each other.*

COLOSSIANS 3:13

Someone once defined insanity as doing the same thing over and over, while expecting a different result. That clearly defined my behavior when it came to pregnancy tests.

As the time drew near each month to see if we had finally become pregnant, madness descended on me like a London fog. I couldn't focus clearly on anything else. My body seemed to explode with sure-fire signs that this month was "it." Every twinge, every emotional outburst, every craving *surely* heralded a positive pregnancy test just around the corner.

And I could never wait for the right day to take the tests. I always began several days in advance and kept taking tests until no doubt remained that I still was not pregnant. My poor husband put up with my insanity — and the blow that our budget suffered at the end of each month as I bought the tests — because he loved me. He understood its importance for me, and although at times he found my behavior irrational (and sometimes just plain silly), he never said a cross word or made me feel badly. Because we're in this together, he put up with stretches of imagination and leaps of faith. I am trying to model his attitude, and extend this grace to others.

These days, I feel much less afraid to have my life disturbed and turned upside down by events and people. Life is messy. People get crazy. Passions and longings that speak of who we are drive all of us. I want my husband, and everyone I love deeply, to become more of who they are by pursuing their dreams, no matter what it costs me or how silly I may think it is.

I want my husband to pursue his wild new business venture, even if it means I have to pinch every penny until it begs for mercy. I want my best friend to pursue the job of her dreams, even if it means she has to move away from me. Infertility has taught me that the greatest sadness can come from being denied your heart's desire and being stopped before you can fulfill a dream. I won't wish that on anyone.

I've learned that dreamers are vulnerable. They walk along, looking at the sky, and it's oh-so-easy to fall and lose heart. If you love a dreamer, get out of their way: Accept their differences. Embrace their passions. Give them the permission to pursue their heart's desire as passionately as you pursue having children.

---

*Lord, thank you for the people in my life who love me*
*enough to let me pursue my dreams. Show me who the*
*dreamers are in my life and how I can encourage them.*
*Help me to keep my mouth shut when I feel critical of*
*someone's passions. Grant me the courage to keep hoping*

*for a child and the strength to continually reach for what
I know may not be there. Let me see this same courage
reflected in those around me, and may You richly bless
us, the dreamers!*

# A DISTANT MEMORY

*A woman giving birth has pain because her time has come;*
*but when her baby is born she forgets the anguish because of her joy*
*that a child is born into the world.*

JOHN 16:21

Sometimes we get so focused on the hardships of infertility that we find it hard to imagine life as anything but spectacular once we win this battle. But consider two sides to the dilemma.

When you win your battle and finally become a parent, your joy probably will help you to forget much of your anguish. Some day, God willing, you will not be able to recall exactly how difficult some moments felt. Your season of longing will fade from memory as surely as old holidays drift away. You will savor the bliss of having a child to love, and your joy will grow even more sweet because of your sorrows.

Yet having a child does not release you from the pain of life. If you set yourself up to feel overjoyed forever once a child joins your family, you may suffer from disappointment. A wise friend, who for years had struggled to conceive, told me after she had given birth that her struggles hadn't ended, they had simply changed. Instead of feeling anxiety and pressure as she watched the months and years tick by without a child, suddenly she felt the anxieties and pressures of rearing a child. And she noticed a sense of disappointment that she felt no tidal wave of relief, just a quiet change of her life's season.

Infertility usually creeps quietly into our lives; much time passes before we even know we have a problem. And just as often, it quietly makes its exit. It may take months before we believe that our season of waiting has ended and we have entered a new season of life. The emotions pent up inside don't burst out, but instead slowly dissipate.

As you pray for the blessing of parenthood, it's wise to pray also for the grace you need to make the transition from this season of life to the next. Just as you savor the occasional moments of joy during your suffering, so give yourself permission to acknowledge the bittersweet moments in victory.

———————

*Lord, when we focus on infertility as the only heartache in life, we become unbalanced. We want to learn to walk by faith, not just because we need it now, but because we'll need it later. When the days seem so dark with the pain and grief of waiting, remind us that this season will pass and someday it will be just a distant memory. Help us to feel at peace in a world of conflicting emotions, where good and bad so often intertwine.*

# IT WOULDN'T HAVE MATTERED

*Yet to all who received him, to those who believed in his name,*
*he gave the right to become children of God —*
*children born not of natural descent . . . but born of God.*

JOHN 1:12-13

After a long battle with infertility, I had a son in the fall of 1999. When the nurses bundled him up and laid him in my arms for the first time, I gazed on his face and out came words that revealed a surprising realization: "It wouldn't have mattered."

I am sure the nurses didn't understand my muttering, but I felt seized with love for this precious infant — not because he came from my womb, but because he came from God.

This little one could do nothing for me and in fact already had caused me countless heartaches. He depended completely on me and would remain a burden, however sweet, for years to come. I loved him because I had gone to hell and back for him. I loved him simply because he *was*. And it "wouldn't have mattered" to me had he been adopted or come from my womb.

Did you know *you* are an adopted child? When God looked down at you He felt seized with an overwhelming love and desire to call you His own. We are not born into His family by natural descent, but by placing our trust in Christ as our hope and Savior. Each of us is adopted into God's kingdom at the moment we receive Christ; each of us receives the right to become His child simply because He loves us.

We depend completely on Him and can offer Him nothing. Already we have caused Him countless heartaches — and yet He yearns to hold us in His arms and call us His children.

God truly is the God of adoptions. Our heavenly Father understands what it is to wait for an adoption and to dream of holding a precious child to call His own. He knows the longing you feel, the ache for your empty arms to be filled. God understands because He has waited for each of us to be adopted into His family. He still waits on many others. He knows better than anyone the hopes, fears, dreams, and heartaches of adoption.

And He waits with longing for you to pour out your heart to Him! He loves you so tenderly and has experienced the ache you feel. You can trust Him as your Savior . . . and you can trust Him with your longing for a child.

---

*Lord, thank you for adopting me into Your family. You have loved each one of us and have patiently waited for each of us to join Your household. We know You have faced many heartaches — and sometimes Your wait must have seemed very long indeed! Lord, You know whether we are considering adoption or eagerly pursuing it. Only You know the challenges we will face and the blessings we'll receive along the way. Since no expert on adoption can compare to You, please guide us and refresh us when we grow tired, and bless our efforts to have a child join our family.*

# NOTES

1. C. S. Lewis, *Mere Christianity* (New York: Touchstone, 1996), p. 172.
2. Barbara Johnson, *Leaking Laffs Between Pampers and Depends* (Nashville: Word Publishing, 2000), p. 56.
3. Gary and Anne Marie Ezzo, *Preparation for Parenting* (Simi Valley: Micah 6:8, 1999), p. 250.
4. Jill Baughan, *A Hope Deferred: A Couple's Guide to Dealing with Infertility* (Portland, Ore.: Multnomah, 1989), pp. 174-175.
5. Baughan, p. 175.

# ABOUT THE AUTHOR

Ginger Garrett is a speaker, workshop leader, and author who loves to share the powerful message of God's intimate involvement in creating and sustaining each new life in the womb, and how we can receive God's strength during the painful trials of life that we will all experience. Her writings have been used by MOPS International, *Christian Women Today,* and the *Atlanta-Journal Constitution.*

Ginger had only been married a few months when she discovered she was pregnant. She was looking forward to a bright future until a devastating car accident took the pregnancy and left her unable to conceive again. She endured countless surgeries and procedures until it was discovered that she would need a corrective surgery that only four doctors in the world had ever performed.

During her moments of pain and confusion, God and His Word became a constant source of encouragement and strength. Her journal entries became the basis for many of the devotions in this book.

Ginger lives in Atlanta, Georgia, with her husband, Mitch, and her two children.

*Private Moments*

# Private Moments

*Private Moments*

From New Life Ministries
founder Steve Arterburn,

*"If you're in trouble,
anytime,
we're here to help…"*

Someone who cares
is always there at
1-800-NEW-LIFE

# Other books in the
# New Life Live! Meditations series.

## Moments for Families of Prodigals

How can you help your son or daughter who has wandered from God? This book helps you claim scriptural promises and shows how you can participate in God's work in your prodigal's life.
**by Robert J. Morgan**
1-57683-473-5

## Moments for Men in the Arena

Encouraging, humorous, and challenging, author Joe Dallas equips today's man to effectively fight the temptations and pressures of his own daily arena.
**by Joe Dallas**
1-57683-539-1
Coming February 2004

## Moments for Singles

Sincere and heartfelt, these insightful devotions challenge singles to live vulnerable, purposeful lives before God.
**by Leigh McLeroy**
1-57683-540-5
Coming February 2004

NAVPRESS ®
BRINGING TRUTH TO LIFE
www.navpress.com

New Life Live! Meditations